Fathers and fatherhood in Britain

Louie Burghes,

Lynda Clarke

and

Natalie Cronin

Occasional Paper 23

FAMILY POLICY STUDIES CENTRE

Published by Family Policy Studies Centre
231 Baker Street, London NW1 6XE

Tel: 0171-486 8179

ISBN 0 907051 99 5

July 1997

The Family Policy Studies Centre is an independent
body which analyses family trends and the impact of
policy. It is a centre of research and information. The
Centre's Governing Council represents a wide
spectrum of political opinion, as well as professional,
academic, church, local authority and other interests.
This Occasional Paper, like all those in the series,
represents the views of the authors and not
necessarily those of the Family Policy Studies Centre.

The Joseph Rowntree Foundation has supported this
project as part of its programme of research and
innovative development projects, which it hopes will
be of value to policy makers and practitioners. The
facts presented and views expressed in this report,
however, are those of the authors and not necessarily
those of the Foundation.

Cover photographs by Format Photographers
Design and print by Intertype

Contents

List of tables

List of figures

List of boxes

Acknowledgements

We should like to thank the Department of Health, the Joseph Rowntree Foundation and the Leverhulme Trust for supporting this project. We are grateful as well for the advice and help provided by the members of the Joseph Rowntree Advisory Committee and by researchers and policy analysts both within and outside the FPSC.

Louie Burghes
Lynda Clarke
Natalie Cronin
Family Policy Studies Centre

Foreword

Fathers and fatherhood in Britain

Fathers and fatherhood have had a bad press in Britain over the last few years. Public discussion has focused in particular on the growing numbers of fathers who live apart from their young children many of whom play a marginal role in their children's lives, financially, socially and emotionally.

We have become concerned too, about what fatherhood means and what a father should be or do. Popular assumptions about the decline of men's breadwinning role conflict with the politicians' concern, over the 1990s, that men take on the financial support of their children. In public policy, breadwinning has been sharply distinguished from nurturing and caring. Yet this distinction is often hard for fathers to see. Instead, for many, financially supporting their families and children is an essential part of the caring that fathers do.

Several competing strands of thought currently exist in Britain about fathers and fathering. Some emphasise the financial, social and psychological consequences both for families and society of fathers' absence from the household or family life. Others focus more on the ways in which fathers are, or are not, changing their roles and becoming more nurturing and caring - in other words 'new men'. A minority view assumes that fathers are increasingly not relevant in the lives of their children and their children's mothers and can be dispensed with.

Much of the discussion is partial and conducted with little regard to the limited research which has been available. But it is also true that informed discussion has been hampered by the absence of social science information, by the relative absence of the voice of fathers themselves and by the lack of an overview of the changing legal position of fathers and our evolving polices towards fatherhood.

Fathers and fatherhood in Britain aims to remedy some of these lacks. It contains exciting and unique demographic analysis of the incidence of fatherhood, telling us for the first time how many men in Britain have fathered a child and where they live in relation to their dependent children. This is the key baseline data which should underpin any serious discussion of fatherhood. The study also charts the changing legal status of fathers and identifies points of conflict in different laws' views of fatherhood. A father's legal state is importantly affected by his marital status although, as is made clear, few fathers and mothers know or understand this.

Fathers' economic role is considered in some detail as this is key to the current preoccupation with failing or changing fatherhood. Often the breadwinning role of fathers has been popularly down played. We hear how 'all families have two-earners now' and an equality of earning power between mothers and fathers is presumed. As this study shows, this is misleading. Men are still the primary breadwinner in the majority of families, a fact which goes a long way to explain why families without fathers in them are much more likely to be poor. And, if breadwinning is still a key component of modern fatherhood, how possible is it for young men to take on the social and legal status of being a father if they have no jobs and poor economic prospects? The economic underpinning of fatherhood should not be ignored.

But fatherhood is, and always has been, about more than just the financial support of families. Fathers have an equally important role in the emotional, social and psychological development of their children and the support of their children's mother. This is more fundamental than sharing the childcare and domestic work, increasingly important though this is, as breadwinning becomes more equitable. Being a father is also about helping young boys and girls develop conceptions of themselves in relation to men as well as women and encouraging them to understand and be comfortable with masculinity and maleness. It is about helping young people understand the dynamics of relationships in general and close relationships in particular. And of course, in sharing parenting with mothers, fathers can both nurture their own children and support mothers who are still the primary carer. The consequences of fathers' being absent from children's lives can, as we show, be severe for children and parents alike.

Well what of fathers and policy? There is no doubt that policy makers have begun to capture dimensions of fathering in their policy net through legislation like the Child Support Act, 1991 and the Criminal Justice Act, 1991. But it is also clear that the policy perspective on fatherhood to date has been partial. Public policy about fathers needs to be more broadly based than just the financial sphere. It needs to be premised on the explicit belief that fathers matter and that society as a whole benefits from good fathering. If more and more men are finding this difficult, then the socio-economic and cultural basis of this difficulty needs tackling. And this may well mean changed tax and benefit policies, as well as better employment opportunities.

Most of all though, talk about fatherhood and fathering cannot be the province only of politicians, journalists and women. Many more men must speak up for their experience and their perspective. What sort of father do they want to be and what needs to be changed to help them? If men do not take responsibility for shaping the public policy debate about fatherhood then they might find themselves increasingly at odds with the prevailing views on what fathers and mothers should do and therefore unable to challenge the structures which constrain them as fathers. We cannot afford to marginalise fathers even further. *Fathers and fatherhood in Britain* is published to inform the important public debate we need to have about fatherhood.

Ceridwen Roberts
Family Policy Studies Centre

1 Introduction

Fathers in the limelight

Fathers and fatherhood are 'in vogue' (Starrels, 1994). After decades when only academics, psychologists and social work professionals paid attention to who fathers were and what they did, now they are prominent on television, in films and advertising and are of apparent interest to the public in general and central to the concerns of policy makers in particular. Indeed, what fathers do – and do not do – is frequently a matter of public and political debate and analysis.

This increasing visibility reflects a pre-occupation with the roles, responsibilities and influence of fathers. It is concerned with the changing attitudes about both what and how much fathering they should or should not do. Today, the active involvement of a father with his children may be expected from birth – if not before – and the *new father* may be expected to take an equal share in parenting within a relationship itself founded on equality. But it would be foolish to assume that such a model is universally supported and it is worth remembering that it is not so long ago that fathers were expected simply to bring in the money, carve the Sunday joint and dispense discipline (Orbach, 1994).

Fatherhood past and present

At least three factors characterise our thinking about the historical role of fathers. First, that their roles were socially accepted and clearly defined. These included providing gender and moral role models for their children both in childhood and into adulthood and making economic provision for their families (McKee and O'Brien, 1982; Kraemer 1988). Secondly, that they wielded a wide-ranging and uncontested authority and were the arbiters of discipline. Finally, that however much or little time fathers spent with their children, it was not expected that it would or should be otherwise.

Such simplification and generalisations mask the diversity of fathers' roles and behaviour (McKee and O'Brien, 1982). Today, more than ever, it may be important to be aware of this. Neither roles nor behaviour are as clearly or definitively socially defined as they once were. Arguably, for a start, there is less consensus about what the role of fathers should be. Is the 'new man' providing equal care with his partner for their children within an equal relationship more than an aspiration for a minority of parents, even if it is increasing in a younger generation? How many parents have succeeded in doing this against severe practical, institutional and cultural constraints – not least those of the labour market? (Hochschild, 1995). Moreover, media hype about new fatherhood may distort reality; we should not presume that it reflects the views of all parents or that none hold more 'traditional' views about family relationships.[1]

The role and position of fathers – like those of mothers – has not been static historically but has evolved over time. What may now seem the 'traditional', and some would say outmoded, image of fatherhood – i.e. breadwinner and gender-role model – itself replaced earlier definitions which in their turn had been subject to change. Kraemer suggests, for example, that the classical father would have regarded it as his duty to train his children for their adult lives; teaching his son a trade and preparing his daughters for marriage (Kraemer, 1993). Until the Infants Custody Act 1839, moreover, the care of children was automatically awarded to the father when families broke down. More generally, his influence and authority were undermined by the rise of professionals – doctors, teachers and magistrates (Kraemer, 1993).

Fathers on fatherhood

Today, as Richards has pointed out, the tendency is to measure the behaviour of fathers with their children by comparison with that of mothers and their children. The agenda of what fatherhood might be is not, therefore, set independently of motherhood or necessarily by fathers (Richards, 1982).

Evidence about what fathers want is limited. Fatherhood still seems popular if the men in the National Child Development Study (NCDS),[2] 33 years old when recently interviewed, are anything to go by; more than 8 in 10 were or wanted to become parents (Ferri, 1994). Moreover, almost a half of the fathers in the survey thought that 'couples who have children should not separate' and two-thirds that 'people should consider the needs of children as more important than their own' (Ferri, 1994). What fathers do, of course, does not necessarily match these ideals.

According to Sianne and Wilkinson (1995) 'younger' fathers (those between 18-34 years) feel their relationships with their children to be warmer and more positive than those they experienced with their fathers. These fathers are said, moreover, to attach less importance to their role and status as breadwinners and more to the nature of their relationship with their partner.

But this is not to argue that fathers in previous generations were uncaring or uninterested in their children. There was probably both more diversity in their relationships with their children than we know about and more social constraints on their taking a more active and/or different role. Moreover, little information is available from fathers about their experience of fatherhood, not least those in 'traditional' two-parent families living with all their own children. Who then is setting the fatherhood agenda and – in the absence of fathers telling their own story – what is the public image of fatherhood?

One current view of the role of fathers holds that it should be much more child-centred and nurturing compared with an earlier model of a more remote financial provider (Hochschild, 1995). This may well reflect the needs of mothers active in the labour market (whether from choice, necessity or both) for greater equality in their relationships with their children's father and a more equal division of domestic chores and child care. Fathers themselves may want a more involved role with their children but find themselves constrained by the increasing demands of their employment.

Fathers face the problem that the world around them is changing – in personal relationships, the domestic domain, family structure, employment and breadwinning – and as a result their role is being redefined and with it the demands made of them (Samuels, 1996). Kraemer (1995d) suggests that *"Men can become participant fathers, as many are increasingly doing, or they can give up the idea of family life and do their best in the outside world. Either way the notion of being the boss at home, is over, probably for ever".*

The public debate

This uncertainty about the role fathers are expected to play and the tension between conflicting definitions of this role, are reflected in recent legislation. While the Children Act 1989 might be thought to reflect the new 'model' fatherhood – emphasising parental responsibility and active parenting – two years later in the Child Support Act 1991 an earlier model of fatherhood – that of economic provider – was dominant. Moreover, it enshrines the view that making financial provision for one's children is of an enduring nature irrespective of changes in the parental relationship or co-residence with children. Recent legislation also reflects an interest in increasing parental, if not specifically paternal, responsibility for their children's behaviour. Provision for doing so is contained within the Criminal Justice Act 1991.

These developments can also be seen as part of a wider anxiety – possibly 'moral panic' – by the government and other commentators about a breakdown in family life as reflected in increasing family separation and divorce, lone-mother families and births outside marriage. The focus here is on the possible demise of the two-parent family, the resulting loss of a central building block of a 'civilised' society (Dennis and Erdos, 1992) and with the *"dismantling of sociological fatherhood"* such that *"all boys and young men without exception … face their future with progressively reducing social pressures or social training to become responsible and competent fathers".* (Dennis, 1993).

Non-resident and 'absent' fathers are seen as leaving boys, in particular, without the necessary role model of a resident father. The consequences are feared to be poorer developmental outcomes, a greater risk of delinquency in adolescence and a greater likelihood of less 'traditional' behaviour patterns in early adulthood, including extra-marital births and cohabitation rather than marriage. Halsey argues that we are witnessing the *"emergence of a new type of young male … who is weakly socialized and weakly socially controlled so far as the responsibilities of spousehood and fatherhood are concerned … he no longer feels the pressure his father and grandfather and previous generations of males felt to be a responsible adult in a functioning community".* (Halsey, 1992).

These developments and debates reflect, in part, the problem oriented nature of social policy. The media too tends to present fathers as either 'heroes' or 'villains' with little serious debate about fatherhood. What debate there is, is said to focus on the *"changing role of men as breadwinners"* but *"the issue of how to reconcile employment and family life was not on the agenda for them"* as it is for mothers (Lloyd, 1995).

Fathers and family change

It is ironic that at a time when more rather than less is expected of fathers in relation to their children, a growing number are living apart from some or all of them: between 1 in 6 and 1 in 7 fathers are not living with all or any of their dependent children (Chapter 2; Ferri, 1994; Haskey, 1994). Family change, both the breakdown of relationships between parents and the formation of subsequent relationships, underlies this. Circumstances other than family change may also separate fathers and their children for extended periods. Some fathers work away from home and some are in prison. Equally, some children live away for extended periods.[3]

Family change not only means that more fathers live apart from their own biological children, but more are also living with children for whom they are social fathers. In 1991, just over one in ten (11 per cent) of the 33 year old fathers interviewed in the NCDS were living with children for whom they were not the biological fathers (Ferri, 1994). Fathers may also have further biological children within their new relationship.

The way fathers fulfil their role with their children may vary and be influenced by the interrelationship between the type of father-child relationship (biological or social), family structure (with biological and/or stepchildren) and whether fathers and their children are living together or apart (see Box below).

Diversity in fatherhood

Fathers living with all and only their own biological children
- in partnership with children's biological mother
- lone father
- in partnership, not children's biological mother

Fathers not living with any biological children (whether or not in contact with them)
- living alone
- living in partnership without children
- living in partnership with stepchildren

Fathers living with some of their biological children
- lone father, or
- living in a partnership with any combination of children from
  - previous partnership
  - stepchildren
  - biological children from current partnership

In other words, to the already existing uncertainty about the role fathers should play with their biological children, a further layer of complexity is added as far as their role with stepchildren is concerned. In addition, fathers' relationships with their biological children may be different when they live with them, compared with when they live apart from one another. Their non-resident fathering may change again when they are also stepfathers to children they live with, and relationships with both their non-resident biological children and their stepchildren may be further altered if fathers have subsequent biological children within their new partnership.

If changes are taking place in the role it is thought fathers should play in 'traditional' nuclear families, it is hardly surprising if there is confusion and uncertainty about what these roles should be in more complex family structures and with children with whom the men do not have a biological tie. The frequently added demands and/or complexities of non-resident and step fathering may mean that fathers are not able to fulfil these roles as they wish.

Similarly, and irrespective of their family structure, the roles fathers play will be influenced and may be curtailed by their psychological, social and economic circumstances. For example, changes which affect the role of fathers are taking place both in the relationships between parents and the labour market and in the labour market itself. Mothers are more likely now to be in employment (Joshi et al, 1995). The changing structure of the labour market – the growth in part-time employment and the service sector – has encouraged this trend while more traditional male employment sectors have declined (Elias and Gregory, 1994). All paid work, moreover, is becoming increasingly insecure and mothers' employment makes a growing contribution to family income (Condy and Roberts, 1994).

There is clearly, then, diversity in fatherhood today, both in terms of family structure and social and economic characteristics. This review cannot do justice to them all, nor to every topic and issue about fathers and fathering. But it is important to remember that most fathering still takes place in intact two-parent first-families, and it is still the case that eight out of ten fathers live with all their biological children (under 18) and three out of four children under 16 years old will not experience their parents' divorce (Chapter 2; Haskey, 1990).

Fatherhood: defining the new diversity

Demographic, social, technological and legal changes have introduced new 'types' of fatherhood – biological and social – for example. There is no universal set of terms to describe the modern diversity of fatherhood. In this report the following terms are used:

biological / natural: a child's genetic father.

social: a man who acts as a father to a child, usually one he lives with, to whom he is not the 'biological' father. Step-fathers are the most common example of 'social' fathers.

absent / present: although the terms 'absent' and 'present' are often used to describe whether a father does or does not live with his children, they refer in this report to whether or not he has contact with some or all of his children.

resident / non-resident: refer to whether a father does or does not live with some or all of his children.

A profile of fathers

Given the current focus on fatherhood it comes as a surprise to find how few regularly published official statistics there are about fathers. Social and economic statistics rarely distinguish between men who are and are not fathers, perhaps because public policy has only recently been so directly concerned with fatherhood. By contrast, government statistics on women commonly tell us whether or not they are mothers, how many children they have and how old their children are.

Structure of the report

The report focuses on the role of fathers in Britain today but some comparisons with Europe are also made. In Section I, Chapter 2 presents original demographic and social data on fathers and fatherhood within the context of family change. Chapter 3 looks at the legal position and status of fathers and recent changes to these. Section II considers *Fatherhood*: fathers' economic role is looked at in Chapter 4, their role in family life in Chapter 5 and children's development and father 'absence' in Chapter 6. Public provision and support for fatherhood is analysed in Chapter 7. The report concludes with a consideration of policy options (Chapter 8).

Notes

1. The 1992 British Social Attitudes Survey, for example, found that just over a half (53 per cent) of the men interviewed thought that it was 'a husband's job to earn the money and a wife's to look after the home and children' (Scott *et al.*, 1993).

2. The NCDS is a longitudinal cohort study of all the children (17,414) born in Great Britain in the week 3-9 March 1958. In addition to their birth details, information about the cohort members has been collected at 7, 11, 16, 23 and 33 years. Analyses from the NCDS are used extensively in the report, notably those by Ferri and Smith (1996).

3. According to the 1991 Census, more than 60,000 dependent children were away at boarding school and more than 22,000 were living in homes or hostels. A further 15,000 were in hospitals or NHS homes (Central Statistical Office, 1994).

2 Who are fathers?
A socio-demographic profile

Lynda Clarke

Men and fatherhood

Fathers in Britain are not an homogeneous group. In talking about their circumstances and role in the family and society we need to be clear about their diversity. The impact of the increasing instability in family life on where fathers and children live, for example, has received little attention. This chapter is concerned with the fertility behaviour of men, the characteristics of fathers and where they and their children live in relation to one another.

To date we have not known how many men become fathers, the ages at which they become fathers, the number of children they knowingly sire (both in and outside marriage) nor the proportion of fathers with two or more families. The characteristics of fathers are included with the birth registration details of their children but only for births to married couples and unmarried couples who jointly-register their babies' births. Information on the fathers of children born outside marriage whose births are registered by the mother alone (now about 15 per cent of all births) is not recorded, so information is not available from this source for all fathers.

Most national surveys in Britain have not asked men if they have ever fathered a child because of the innate validity problems: men can conceal parenthood or may even not know about conceptions. While national statistics on men's marriages and partnerships are available, the same is not true of fatherhood. For example, it is not known how many men father children prior to marriage, in cohabiting relationships, in first or subsequent marriages or outside relationships. In addition, little information is available on fathers' economic, social or personal characteristics, because it has not been possible to identify fathers as a group.

Note

Initial analysis for this chapter was undertaken by Lynda Clarke, Ann Condy and Adrian Downing at the FPSC and was funded by the Department of Health (Clarke *et al.*, 1995). Subsequent analyses were undertaken by Lynda Clarke and Georgia Verropoulou at City University as part of a project funded by the Leverhulme Trust. Table 2.12 was derived by Andrew Sloggett and Lynda Clarke at the London School of Hygiene and Tropical Medicine.

Data on fatherhood: *British Household Panel Study (BHPS)*

The demography of fatherhood is becoming internationally topical.[1] There is, however, very little recent evidence on male fertility from any country, with the exception of Denmark (Coleman, 1995). The availability of retrospective fertility and marital histories for men as well as women in the second wave (1992) of the British Household Panel Study (BHPS) presents a novel opportunity to begin to answer some questions about British fathers.

The BHPS is the first national sample survey to ask men of all ages about any children they have fathered. It is more comprehensive than a cohort survey (such as the 1958 cohort in the NCDS) as it covers men of all ages. This information allows a comparison of men who are fathers with those who are not, and an examination of the characteristics of fathers both at the time of the interview and at the birth of their children. It allows changes in fathers' relationships since first fatherhood to be traced, as well any subsequent paternities.

Any data on male fertility will be subject to omissions. The breakdown in parenting partnerships and child-bearing outside partnerships create the potential for considerable under-reporting of male fertility, both deliberate and unwitting, when men do not live with children. A recent assessment of the reliability of the fertility reports by men showed that under-reporting of fertility of men in the surveys studied runs to between 10% and 15% of all births, and to between 30% and 50% of non-marital births.[2] The overall estimates for children of all ages of under-reporting of men's fertility in the BHPS are 10% for all births and 35% for births outside marriage. Under-reporting by men of marital births in which the marital union had dissolved prior to the survey runs as high as 35% in Britain (Rendall *et al.*, 1996). The 1992 round of the BHPS has been used to examine the demography of fathers in Britain presented here. Details of the survey have been documented elsewhere (Buck *et al.*, 1994). Wave 2 of the BHPS included a marital, cohabitation and fertility history for both men and women. From this data the proportion of men who report that they have had children and the proportion of these fathers who are currently living with their children have been estimated. Nevertheless, detailed analysis of the BHPS is somewhat restricted by the relatively small numbers of fathers in the dataset. Out of a total of 4,350 men, just 2,664 have ever fathered a child and around half of these (1,379) are fathers of dependent children, defined as under the age of 18.

This chapter looks first at the characteristics of men who are fathers compared with those who are not, and then presents a demographic profile of fatherhood (the ages at which men become fathers and the characteristics of fathers). Finally it examines where fathers live in relation to their children and their family situation.

Men and parental status

This section examines characteristics of men according to whether they report that they have fathered children or not. It is therefore dependent on men reporting themselves as fathers and any fatherhood that is undetected, undeclared or perhaps even unknown to the man himself will be excluded.

Age and parental status

Table 2.1 shows that, understandably, the older men are the more likely they are to be fathers. The proportion of men who are fathers is lower than the proportion of women at all ages (except for a statistically insignificant difference at 50–59 years) and is particularly different below the age of 35. This is evidence of the later age of parenthood for men than for women. Just 1% of teenage men are fathers, compared with 5% of teenage women. In fact nearly 3 in 10 men in their late thirties have still never fathered a child.

Table 2.1	Parental status of men and women by age (weighted)*			
Age group	Mothers	All women	Fathers	All men
	(%)	(N)	(%)	(N)
16-19	5.3	299	1.2	336
20-24	25.0	460	10.6	413
25-29	50.8	541	37.2	440
30-34	72.3	520	58.4	480
35-39	79.6	435	71.8	405
40-44	88.3	474	80.2	386
45-49	88.9	453	85.9	395
50-59	86.8	613	87.2	563
60-69	81.2	602	74.8	497
70+	82.2	671	81.5	435
Total (N)	3525	5068	2664	4350

* Percentages in all the tables have been weighted to account for sampling error. Total numbers shown (N) are actual numbers of men and women interviewed.

Population: men and women aged 16 and over. *Source: BHPS 1992*

Turning to the older age groups, the overall childless rate for men is around 14%, with the exception of the 60–69 age group, that is men born in the 1920s, whose overall rate of childlessness is nearly one-quarter. These are the cohorts of men who would have been in their prime family formation years during the Second World War. It is interesting that, contrary to expectation given the longer male fertile life, more men are childless than women at all ages (again with the exception of the 50–59 age group). This confirms evidence from the 1946 cohort study in Britain and from Denmark which also shows a higher level of childlessness among men than women (Coleman, 1995).

Marital status at interview

Fathers were more likely than mothers to be currently married at the time of the BHPS interview (Table 2.2). This mainly reflects the fact that mothers were more likely than fathers to be widowed because of women's greater longevity than men. However, mothers were also more likely to be divorced, separated or never married than fathers. Women and men who were not parents had similar marital status distributions to each other, with over half never having married by the time of the interview.

Table 2.2	Men's and women's marital status by parental status (weighted)					
Marital status	Mothers	Fathers	Non-mothers	Non-fathers	Total women	Total men
	(%)	(%)	(%)	(%)		
Married	65.6	83.2	27.0	24.6	2776	2609
Living as couple	4.0	4.9	11.7	10.4	351	334
Widowed	17.6	4.7	6.2	1.6	630	144
Divorced	7.3	4.6	1.9	1.5	295	157
Separated	2.7	1.5	0.7	0.7	113	56
Never married	2.8	1.0	52.5	61.2	905	1050
Total (N)	3525	2664	1545	1686	5070	4350

Population: all adults 16 and over.   Source: BHPS 1992

Most fathers – more than 8 in 10 – were married at the time of the survey. By comparison, only a quarter of men who reported they were not fathers at the interview were married. This difference is partly, but not entirely, explained by the age difference between fathers and non-fathers, with fathers tending on average to be older than men who had not yet had children. However, looking just at men between the ages of 30 and 44, fewer than 4 in 10 of the non-fathers were married compared with over 8 in 10 of the fathers (data available from author). Remarriage in part explains the higher marriage rate among fathers; 13% of all fathers and 10% of non-fathers who were currently married were re-married. In most cases these only involved second marriages; just 1% of currently married fathers had been married three times (Clarke et al., 1995).

Fathers were correspondingly less likely to be cohabiting than non-fathers. Just 5% of fathers were cohabiting compared with 10% of non-fathers. Cohabitation was more prevalent among fathers below the age of 30 (although it should be borne in mind that the numbers sampled in this study were very small). Just under 4 in 10 of 20 to 24-year-old fathers and 17% of the 25 to 29-year-old fathers were currently cohabiting (Clarke et al., 1995). More fathers who were currently cohabiting had previously been married than cohabiting non-fathers (Clarke et al., 1995). Again, as with the marriage rate, this difference is partly a function of age; the generally younger age profile of the non-fathers means that they were less likely to have been married.

Economic activity

Men and women have different employment patterns. The difference is more pronounced among parents. Mothers are less likely to be in paid employment (taking the self-employed and employed together in Table 2.3a) than fathers or non-parents. Fathers of dependent children have the highest employment rates: 85% of fathers of dependent children (aged below 18) were employed compared with 71% of fathers whose children were all over 18 and 68.5% of men who were not parents (Tables 2.3a and 2.3b).

Table 2.3a **Economic activity of women and men by parental status (weighted)**

Economic activity	Mothers	Fathers	Non-mothers	Non-fathers	Total women	Total men
	(%)	(%)	(%)	(%)		
Self-employed	5.1	17.3	2.6	9.3	172	502
Employed	53.5	62.3	65.9	59.2	2363	2241
Unemployed	3.4	9.2	5.9	11.5	164	371
Retired	6.1	4.5	4.1	2.1	190	115
Family care	28.0	0.3	2.5	-	805	8
Maternity leave	0.1	-	0.1	-	3	-
Full-time student, school	0.7	0.3	16.0	14.3	266	251
Long-term sick, disabled	2.9	5.9	2.1	2.7	100	161
Govt. training scheme	0.1	0.2	0.4	0.7	9	17
Other	0.1	0.0	0.4	0.2	9	3
Total (N)	2728	2127	1353	1542	4081	3669

Population: adults aged 16-64. _Source: BHPS 1992_

It is interesting to compare these findings with the analysis by Harrop and Moss (1994) of men's economic activity by parental status. They found higher proportions in employment overall in 1989 (three years earlier than the BHPS data was collected): 89% of fathers and 72% of men without children in employment. This difference might be explained partly by the smaller sample size of the BHPS and by the fact that unemployment was a few percentage points higher in 1992 than it had been in 1989.[3]

A higher proportion of men who are not parents were students than was the case for fathers, and this is because more of them are younger (Table 2.3a). Similarly, the higher proportion of fathers of children over 18 who are retired is because these fathers are themselves older (Table 2.3b).

Table 2.3b **Economic activity of fathers and mothers by whether they have dependent children (weighted)**

Economic activity	With dependent children		No dependent children	
	Mothers	Fathers	Mothers	Fathers
	(%)	(%)	(%)	(%)
Self-employed	4.9	16.9	5.2	17.6
Employed	53.4	67.8	53.7	53.4
Unemployed	3.3	10.4	3.5	7.3
Retired	-	0.3	14.3	11.4
Family care	35.5	0.5	18.0	-
Maternity leave	0.1	-	-	-
Full-time student, school	1.2	0.4	0.1	-
Long-term sick, disabled	1.3	3.3	4.9	10.2
Govt training scheme	0.2	0.3	-	0.1
Other	0.1	0.1	0.3	-
Total (N)	1665	1379	1061	740

Population: parents aged 16-64 with dependent children under age of 18 years.

Source: BHPS 1992

Men in the United Kingdom work the longest hours of all male employees in Europe (Eurostat, 1996; this excludes self-employment, the inclusion of which would increase working hours in other countries). Moreover, fathers who are working are likely to work extremely long hours (Ferri and Smith, 1996). Patterns of paid work in families and hours of work and domestic roles are examined in detail in Chapters 4 and 5.

Social class

The social class of parents at the time of interview does not differ greatly from that of people who are not parents, although men are more likely than women to be in the higher social classes, according to the Registrar-General's classification. The figures in Table 2.4 show, for example, that only a slightly higher proportion of fathers come from professional, managerial, technical and skilled manual occupations than do non-fathers. Conversely, a higher proportion of non-fathers than fathers are in skilled non-manual, partly-skilled manual and unskilled occupations. There may also be a link for men between education and age at onset of parenthood, such as is known to exist for women. Men who had fathered children at a younger age were more likely to be engaged in manual occupations at the time of the interview and less likely to be in skilled work than men who began their families in their late thirties and forties (Clarke *et al.*, 1995). Data on educational level at the time of first parenthood is needed, however, to establish this link irrefutably.

Social class	Mothers	Fathers	Non-mothers	Non-fathers	Total women	Total men
Table 2.4	**Men's and women's social class by parental status (weighted)**					
	(%)	(%)	(%)	(%)		
Professional	1.4	8.5	3.9	7.7	59	228
Managerial & Technical	26.8	31.0	28.0	24.6	738	802
Skilled non-manual	36.0	12.0	45.1	17.8	1028	394
Skilled manual	9.2	34.4	8.6	29.9	240	916
Partly-skilled manual	17.7	11.6	12.9	16.0	413	373
Unskilled	8.9	2.5	1.5	4.0	153	90
Total (N)	1619	1696	1012	1107	2631	2803

Population: adults aged 16-64.   Source: BHPS 1992

Fatherhood

The next two sections present the demographic profile of fatherhood. They include the ages at which men have children, the number of children they father and how their fatherhood behaviour relates to their socio-demographic characteristics.

Age of fatherhood

Table 2.5 presents the results of an initial analysis of men's fertility history. This provides information on the age of fathers at the birth of their first child and any subsequent children. About one third of fathers became fathers for the first time when they were still under the age of 25, and the most common age at which fathers had their first child was 25–29 (4 in 10 had their first child between these ages). Fathers are older on average than mothers at first and subsequent births. Women are more likely to be teenage mothers than men are to be teenage fathers (13% of mothers compared with 3% of fathers were teenagers at the birth of their first child) (Clarke *et al.*, 1996a). However, both fathers and mothers in this country are less likely to be teen parents than in the USA (Clarke *et al.*, 1996a). Previous research has examined longitudinal evidence on teenage fatherhood in this country from the 1958 cohort and found that early fatherhood was associated with boys whose families experienced financial hardship (Dearden *et al.*, 1994).

Table 2.5 **Percentage of fathers by age at birth and birth order (weighted)**

Age group	Birth order					Total births
	1st	**2nd**	**3rd**	**4th**	**5th+**	
16-19	3.4	0.7				107
20-24	30.8	13.9	5.6	2.4	1.8	1159
25-29	40.5	39.5	31.0	19.4	8.4	2163
30-34	18.5	31.4	34.1	39.5	16.3	1511
35-39	4.9	11.6	21.8	23.7	36.3	662
40-44	1.2	2.3	5.7	10.2	21.0	191
45+	0.7	0.6	1.8	4.8	16.2	81
Total children (N)	2586	1975	838	312	163	5874

Population: all fathers aged 16 and over. *Source: BHPS 1992*

About 7 in 10 fathers who had a second child did so between the ages of 25 and 34. Fewer men go on to have more children but, of those that do, the most common age at the birth of a third child is also between 25 and 34, and over 30 for higher-order births.

Average family size

The average number of children reported by fathers was lower than that reported by mothers at each age (Table 2.6). This either means that men have fewer children than women at each age, that they are under-reporting the number of children they have fathered, or that the survey is missing fathers more than mothers due to death or omission.

Table 2.6 **Average family size for mothers and fathers by age**

Age group	Mothers	Total	Fathers	Total
16-19	1.071	14	1.000	4
20-24	1.550	109	1.378	45
25-29	1.849	284	1.667	168
30-34	2.211	379	1.968	283
35-39	2.275	349	2.238	294
40-44	2.355	422	2.347	317
45+	2.505	1968	2.458	1553
Total (N)		3525		2664

Population: all parents aged 16 and over. *Source: BHPS 1992*

It is true that men have children at older ages on average than women, so part of the difference at younger ages could be due to the different age distributions of men and women at birth. However, this should even out at the older ages, whereas, even at age 45, a slight difference remains. The fact that differences persist suggest that fatherhood is under-reported, as discussed earlier.

Partnership at birth of children

Most children reported by men were born within marriage (93%). Less than 1 in 10 of all children were born outside marriage – 4% outside a co-residential relationship, 2% in a cohabiting relationship and only 1% in a cohabitation where the parents had married before the interview (Table 2.7).

Table 2.7	**Fathers by union status at birth and birth order of child (weighted)**					
			Birth order %			All children
Type of union	1st	2nd	3rd	4th	5th+	
Marriage	90.6	96.1	95.0	92.9	91.5	93.30
Premarital cohabitation	1.6	0.7	1.2	1.0	3.0	1.2
Cohabitation	2.2	1.4	1.6	2.9	2.4	1.9
Outside relationship	5.6	1.8	2.2	3.2	3.1	3.6
Total children (N)	2568	1962	831	305	164	5830

Population: all fathers aged 16 and over.   *Source: BHPS 1992*

These results may at first sight appear contrary to recent trends of increased child-bearing outside marriage, but it must be remembered that the fathers in this sample cover all ages. Some of the children of these men would have been born some time ago, when births outside marriage were not common. Again, the under-reporting of births may be a part of the explanation (Rendall *et al.*, 1996). This under-reporting is more noticeable, moreover, for earlier periods when births outside marriage were less generally accepted or perhaps more likely to be 'forgotten' because of the passage of time (Rendall *et al.*, 1996). Thus, a much higher proportion of recent births were reported as being born outside marriage, nearly 17% of births reported between 1986 and 1991 – 7.5% being born in a cohabiting relationship, 4% in a premarital cohabitation and 4.5% outside a relationship (data not shown in table).

This is consistent with findings from the 1958 cohort study, where both fathers and, to a lesser extent, mothers were found to under-report births when interviewed at the age of 33 when they had mentioned births at a previous interview at the age of 23. The 'forgetting' of births usually occurred where a child had died or been separated from the parent (Di Salvo *et al.*, 1996).

It is interesting, but not surprising, that the proportion of first births inside marriage reported by men is lower than for subsequent births. A higher proportion of first births than subsequent births reported by fathers occurred when they were not living with the other parent. These parents may live together at a later stage. We know from the 1958 cohort survey that some fathers move in with the mother and child at some stage after the birth of the child (Clarke *et al.*, 1997). Fathers may, of course, start living with another partner with whom they have further children.

Educational status

Table 2.8 **Fathers by age at birth of first child and current educational status (weighted)**

| Age group | Highest educational qualification% | | | | | All Fathers |
	Degree	A-Level	O-Level	Appren-ticeship	None	(N)
16-19	18.5	7.1	36.9	3.7	33.8	92
20-24	19.5	10.0	23.1	8.3	39.1	811
25-29	33.4	9.7	19.3	7.1	30.5	1034
30-34	36.7	11.5	16.2	8.0	27.6	463
35-39	40.8	12.4	10.4	10.0	26.4	126
40-44	22.0	18.2	12.6	8.4	38.8	31
45+	30.1	0.0	13.5	0.0	56.4	15
All ages (N)	767	276	534	186	809	2572

Population: all fathers aged 16 and over.   *Source: BHPS 1992*

Fathers' age at first birth and their educational level at the time of the BHPS interview is shown in Table 2.8. In general, the younger fathers are at the birth of their first child, the lower is their highest educational qualification. However, it is clear that an early age at fatherhood is not as prohibitive to obtaining higher education for men as it is for women (Clarke *et al.*, 1996a). Around 19% of men who first fathered a child below the age of 25 had a degree at the time of the interview compared with 10% of women who became mothers under 25 years (data for mothers not shown).

Residential status and family situation of fathers

We now turn to whether fathers are living with or apart from their children. Who are the fathers who are parted from their children? How many families with children are absent fathers parted from? How many have formed new families?

A father's likelihood of living apart from a child increases with the child's age. This is because the older the child the longer the family is exposed to the risk of separation and children usually stay living with their mother after family break-up. In the analysis reported below, fathers' residence status relative to child(ren) was calculated only where children were under 18. This does not necessarily indicate that the father does not have additional children over the age of 18. Eighteen rather than 16 was chosen as the age of dependence for children because most children now remain in the parental home until this age. Also, it could be argued that this is the age of financial dependence as far as state benefits are concerned. Results based on children under 16 years showed similar patterns to the results presented here (Clarke *et al.*, 1995).

Fathers living with or apart from their children

Most fathers reside with their children. When they live apart from their children they are no more likely to be living apart from girls than boys. Table 2.9 shows that

- more than 4 out of every 5 fathers (85%) live with all their child(ren) under the age of 18;
- more than 1 out of every 8 (13%) fathers of children under the age of 18 were not living with any of their children and
- a further 1 out of every 40 (2.5%) of fathers were living with only some of their dependent children.

It might be hypothesised that the higher number of children a man fathers the greater the risk that he will live apart from those children. However, it is fathers of only one child who are least likely to be living with their child; nearly 1 in 5 of these men were not doing so (19%). This is because eldest children are more likely than subsequent ones to be born to unmarried parents who are not living together.

Fathers who do not live with any of their children are more likely to be separated or divorced and more likely to be never married than men who live with their children (Clarke *et al.*, 1996a). Only one-quarter of fathers who were not co-resident with any of their children were married, compared with over nine-tenths (94%) of fathers living with all their children and over a half (59%) of fathers living with some of their children.

Fathers who live with only some of their childen include men who have had children in second relationships and whose children born in a previous relationship remain with their mother. The largest percentage of fathers who live with some but not all of their children under the age of 18 was fathers with 5 or more children, although the number of these fathers is very small (Table 2.9). They are, also, more likely to be cohabiting than men who live with all or none of their children.

Table 2.9 **Residential status of fathers by number of children under 18**							
Residential status	**Number of children under 18**					**Total**	
of father	1	2	3	4	5+	Number /	%
Living with all own children under 18	80.7	90.1	86.2	87.2	40.9	1168 / 84.8%	
Living with some of own children under 18	-	2.4	4.8	11.5	47.4	35 / 2.5%	
Not living with any of own children under 18	19.3	7.5	9.0	1.3	11.7	174 / 12.6%	
Total number (N)	543	586	192	45	11	1377	
% of fathers	39.4%	42.6%	13.9%	3.3%	0.8%	100%	
Population: fathers with children aged under 18 years.					*Source: BHPS 1992*		

Housing tenure is often taken as an indicator of social or economic advantage or disadvantage. Fathers who live apart from some or all of their children are more likely than fathers who live with all of their children to live in the less advantaged situations: in either local authority or privately rented accommodation (Table 2.10). However, it is unclear from current data whether this disadvantage exists prior to, or as a result of, being parted from children. Data on circumstances prior to separation are necessary to unravel this relationship.

Fathers who do not live with any of their children are three times more likely than fathers living with all of their children, and nearly eight times more likely than fathers living with only some of their children, to have accommodation in the privately-rented sector. It should be noted, however, that the total number of fathers living in this housing sector is relatively small.

Further analyses of fathers' residential status relative to their children suggest that fathers who are not living with children are materially disadvantaged (e.g. in income, socio-economic group, and car access) compared with fathers who are living with all of their children (Clarke *et al.*, 1995). However, without longitudinal data it is impossible to disentangle whether this is a cause or consequence of family breakdown, or linked to both or to some other factors.

Table 2.10 **Tenure status by residential status of fathers in Great Britain**

Residential status	Tenure status			Total (N)
	Owner-Occupier	Local Authority	Private Rented	
	%	%	%	
Not living with any of own children	55.0	29.5	15.5	174
Living with all own children under 18	77.1	17.9	5.0	1168
Living with some of own children under 18	60.3	37.7	2.0	35
Total (N)	1017	264	96	1377

Population: fathers with children aged under 18 years. *Source: BHPS 1992*

The risk of absent fatherhood

To what extent do the combined effects of the father's age, socio-economic background and type of parental relationship that a child was born into and the length of that relationship affect the risk that the father will live away from his child(ren)?

The results of logistic regression modelling of the BHPS data on children under the age of 18 reported by fathers are shown in Table 2.11. These show the risks of children being separated from fathers according to their father's characteristics. Odds ratios above 1 mean the group is more likely to be separated from a father with that characteristic

Table 2.11 **Odds ratios of the risk of children being separated from fathers according to father's characteristics**

Age Group	Model 1	Model 2	Model 3	Model 4	Model 5
16-19	4.03**	1.54	1.27	1.41	1.32
20-24	1.70**	1.55*	1.35	1.32	1.21
25-29	1.00	1.00	1.00	1.00	1.00
30-34	0.52**	0.56**	0.56**	0.56**	0.60*
35-39	0.49*	0.52*	0.51*	0.51*	0.52*
40-44	0.66	0.55	0.53	0.57	0.62
45+	1.33	0.99	0.91	0.95	1.02
Birth Relationship					
Marriage		1.00	1.00	1.00	1.00
Cohabitation		2.76**	2.31**	2.22*	1.85
No relationship		13.05**	12.7**	11.96**	9.28**
Housing Tenure					
Owner-Occupier			1.00	1.00	1.00
Local Authority			1.58*	1.47	1.39
Private Rented			2.56**	2.49**	2.50**
Vehicle Access					
Access				1.00	1.00
No access				2.08**	1.93*
Relationship Length					
0-5 years					2.74**
5-10 years					3.08**
10-15 years					2.38**
15-25 years					1.00
25 or more					0.75
-2*Log Likelihood	1309.71	1221.56	1206.76	1199.28	1171.97

* significance level <0.05; **significance level <0.01   Sample size: 2,139

Population: children aged under 18 years

Source: BHPS 1992. Analysed by L. Clarke and G. Verroupolou

when compared with the baseline category (shown as 1.00). The results in the first model suggest that there is an increase in the risk of fathers not living with their child if the child is born to a teenage father (Clarke and Verropoulou, 1996). This apparent increase, however, did not continue when the type of relationship was taken into account in model 2, thus suggesting that it is the type of relationship between the father and mother rather than the age of the father that is the major explanatory factor. The type of relationship at birth remains important even when other factors are held constant in models 3 and 4.

Cohabitation disappears from statistical significance in model 5 because relationship length is entered in the model. Cohabitation at the time of the child's birth in model 2 suggests an increased risk of later parting from the child (of around two-and-three-quarter times) compared with the risk for married fathers. However, the highest risk, not surprisingly, is for fathers who are not co-resident with the child's mother at the time of birth (around 13 times more likely than for married fathers). There is also evidence of material disadvantage (tenure and car access) being linked to absent fatherhood, but it could be argued that housing tenure could be a consequence rather than cause of separation.

Family situation of fathers

It is important for policy purposes to know the pattern of fathers' residence in relation to their children – i.e. living with and apart from them – and their subsequent partnering and fathering behaviour. To this end a longitudinal picture of the family situation of fathers has been derived by linking their fertility and relationship histories. To do this a scheme of family situation has been devised by counting commitments or responsibilities. The clock starts when a man first fathers a child; he then has one commitment. If he fathers further children in that same co-residential relationship he still has only one family situation or commitment. However, if he parts from that family he then has two family situations or commitments, regardless of whether he is on his own or in another relationship, because he is separated from the child(ren) in his first family. In other words, only living with a child or leaving a family with a child counts as a commitment or family situation. If a father forms a second relationship after leaving his first family but this second relationship also breaks down, then he will be in a further, third, family or commitment situation only if he has fathered a child in this second relationship from whom he is parted.

Information on fathers' family situation, which has not been known to date, is shown in Table 2.12 for men who have children under the age of 18. It shows whether fathers are living with their child(ren) under the age of 18, whether they are in a co-residential union or not at the time of the interview and how many family situations or commitments they have. Note that family situation includes children of all ages, not just children under the age of 18, as commitments do not stop at 18 and most of the older children would not be much older than 18.

Only a minority of fathers had very complicated family histories. The bottom row of Table 2.12 shows that
- nearly three-quarters of fathers were in their first family situation, in other words with only one family commitment;
- nearly one-quarter (23%) had two family commitments, but the majority of these were men who were parted from their first family and now living on their own;
- only 3% had three or more family commitments.

Most fathers (73%) were in their first family situation and living with all of their children under the age of 18. In total, 84% of fathers were living with all of their children but 5% were living on their own as lone fathers and 6% were in subsequent relationships.

Table 2.12 **Family situation of fathers by whether living with children and current relationship status**

Residence and relationship status		1 %	2 %	3 %	4 %	5 %	6 %	Total (N) / %
Family situation / commitments								
With all own child(ren)								
- *in relationship*		73.0	6.1	*	-	-	-	1095 / 79.2%
- *on own*		-	4.3	0.7	*	-	-	71 / 5.1%
With some of own child(ren)								
- *in relationship*		0.2	1.7	*	-	-	-	27 / 1.9%
- *on own*		-	0.3	0.7	-	-	-	14 / 1.0%
With none of own child(ren)								
- *in relationship*		0.6	2.8	0.2	-	-	*	66 / 4.8%
- *on own*		-	7.7	1.3	-	-	-	109 / 7.9%
All fathers of children	N	1020	318	41	2		1	1382
under 18	%	73.8	23.0	3.0		0.2		100%

* = below 0.1%
Population: fathers with children aged under 18 years.

Source: BHPS 1992. Derived by A. Sloggett and L. Clarke

More than 1 in 10 fathers (13%) were not living with any of their children under the age of 18 and most of these fathers (9%) were living on their own, 10% of whom (1.2% of all fathers) had fathered children in two families. A much smaller proportion of fathers – only 3% – were living with only some of their children under the age of 18. Most of these fathers were living on their own.

Findings from the 1958 NCDS are consistent with the results reported here. The evidence from the NCDS, whose cohort members were last interviewed in 1991, is that two-thirds (66%) of men were fathers by the age of 33 and the great majority of these fathers (85%) had all their children living with them (Ferri, 1993).

Conclusion

This chapter aimed to examine the parental status of men, the pattern of fathering of children and the family situation of fathers using the 1992 BHPS. The present analysis is the first study to estimate the lifetime parenting experience of a nationally representative sample of men in Britain, apart from cohort studies. It compares men who are fathers with those who are not and then describes fathers' characteristics both at the time of the interview and at the time of the birth of any children.

It examines, as well, parental status as reported by men, their pattern of fathering and the family history of fathers, including whether they are living with their children.

Men as parents

Fatherhood is less common for young men than motherhood is for young women and there appear to be cohort differences in the proportion of men reporting themselves as childless. Fathers are more likely than other men to be married but non-fathers are more likely to be cohabiting. Fathers were more likely to be employed than other men, but these differences in economic status reflect differences in the age profile of fathers and non-fathers.

Fatherhood

One-third of fathers had their first child when they were under 25 years old and of those who had a second child over two-thirds did so between the ages of 25 and 34. More than 9 in every 10 children were born to men who were married.

Family situation of fathers

Family breakdown is reflected in the finding that 13% of men who report themselves as fathers of children under the age of 18 were not living with any of their children and a further 3% were living with only some of their dependent children.[4] Nearly three-quarters of men (73%) who reported being fathers of children under the age of 18 were living in their first family with their children. Overall, over four-fifths (84%) of fathers lived with all their children under the age of 18 but 5% were living as lone fathers and 6% were in second or subsequent relationships. This study shows that only a small minority of fathers have children in more than one family, even after allowing for under-reporting of births by men.

Men who fathered a child in their teens would be less likely to be living with the child's mother, but this was accounted for by the type of parental relationship at the birth of the child. Thus, cohabitation of parents at the birth of a child suggests an increased risk that the father would be absent at a later stage. The highest risk of being absent from a child, not surprisingly, is found for fathers who were not co-resident with the mother at the birth of the child. We know from the 1958 cohort study, however, that a proportion of fathers who are not resident with the mother at the birth of a child are likely to live with them at some later stage (Clarke et al., 1997).

Further research

The numbers of men in the BHPS limit the examination of certain questions. For example, the trend in childlessness for men in recent cohorts would be worthy of further investigation given the evidence from Danish data that men are becoming more likely than women to be childless at younger ages. Whether this is a delay in the start of fathering children or an avoidance altogether is not clear. It would be interesting, also, to follow trends for recent cohorts, i.e. younger men, in relationship status at birth as the risk of men not being co-resident with their children is highly linked to partnership status at birth.

There are many more questions to be addressed when assessing the standpoint of fathers in the current debate over fathers' obligations and roles in the changing family scenario. Although we cannot answer many of these questions definitively because of a lack of national data, this work begins to establish a demographic backcloth for a detailed picture of fatherhood in Britain.

Notes

1. For example, the International Union for the Scientific Study of Population held a meeting on 'Fertility and the Male Life Cycle in the Era of Fertility Decline', in Zacatecas, Mexico, on 13-16 November 1995. The demography of fatherhood was selected, as well, as the theme of a session for the Population Association of America in the spring of 1997.

2. This study compared the data from the BHPS with that from a panel study from the United States, the Panel Study of Income Dynamics. It assembled evidence from both panel studies on underreporting from 1980 to 1991 by comparing male and female survey fertility histories to each other and to birth registration data (Rendall *et al.*, 1996).

3. According to the Labour Force Survey, 7.3% of men were unemployed (according to the International Labour Force definition) compared with 11.5% in 1992 (*Employment Gazette*, June 1995).

4. There would be some increase in the proportion of fathers found to be not living with any of their children if account were taken of the under-reporting of fatherhood.

3 The law relating to fathers

Natalie Cronin

The changing law of fatherhood

This chapter describes the current law relating to fathers and fatherhood and recent changes to it. It is a snapshot of a changing picture, in part the result of pressure for legal reform, often reflecting changes in society at large. Contradictions in the current laws relating to fatherhood are considered and aspects of the law which seem problematic for fathers today are identified.

There are wider issues about the development of the law relating to fatherhood which are not dealt with here. Not least among these is the influence of historical concepts of masculinity and the legal sanctioning of married heterosexual relationships in which the father is the financial provider (Collier, 1995). Neither are the changing ideals and expectations of fatherhood as exemplified in law examined (see, for example, Sarre, 1996).

Who is the child's father?

The married man

A married man is presumed in law to be the father of children born to his wife although he may challenge this. Evidence from scientific tests and birth registration are available for determining parentage (Box page 34).

The unmarried father

Changes in social attitudes, including more liberal views about illegitimacy, culminated in the Family Law Reform Act 1987. The Act removed almost all legal disadvantages suffered by illegitimate children and ended the distinction between them and those born legitimate.

But as far as fathers were concerned, a distinction remained between those who were and were not married. The Law Commission, which produced two reports on illegitimacy (in 1982 and 1986) prior to the passing of the Family Law Reform Act, was initially in favour of abolishing illegitimacy. This would have placed unmarried fathers in the same position as their married counterparts.

Evidence for determining parentage

Scientific tests

A court can direct the use of blood tests in any civil proceedings in which parentage is in question, whether any of the parties have applied for the test or not. The court may only direct tests, it cannot order a party to provide a sample. Inferences may be drawn from refusal to participate. Past cases show the difficulty in deciding whether to resort to testing in cases where making a finding as to parentage would disrupt a stable family relationship. However, discovering the truth has generally been granted more weight than preserving the legitimacy of the child, even when this leaves the child with no known father. The choice between the different tests lies with the applicant. Blood tests can only determine conclusively whether a person is **not** the child's parent, although it can also indicate probability of paternity. DNA profiling can establish parentage with virtual certainty, but is much more expensive.

Birth registration

This is an important way of establishing parentage, since entry of the name of a particular man as the child's father in the register is *prima facie* evidence that he is the father. The onus of proof is on anyone who wishes to dispute the matter.

By law, the mother and father of any child born in England and Wales must, within 42 days of the birth inform the Registrar of Births. An unmarried father is not under this duty. The informant is asked to state the name of the child's father and it will be recorded without any further evidence if he is the mother's husband. If the couple are not married the father's name can only appear in one of three cases:

- where the couple jointly request registration (either by personal attendance before the registrar or by providing a statutory declaration of paternity with the mother's acknowledgement of it);

- by providing evidence of a parental responsibility agreement, or

- by providing evidence of a parental responsibility order or an order for financial provision for the child. Either parent therefore can have the child's name registered without the consent of the other providing that a court order is obtained.

If the father's name is not known or where the unmarried father does not attend the birth registration, the relevant space is left blank. However, the birth may be re-registered later, if for example, the couple marry or a declaration of parentage is made.

Judicial procedures for determining parentage

A court may have to adjudicate on parentage for a number of reasons, such as inheritance, in divorce proceedings involving adultery, or to grant a parental responsibility order. If the court makes a finding of paternity it is binding and provides *prima facie* evidence which would need to be rebutted in any subsequent proceedings.

A person may also apply to the court for a declaration that a given person is or was his father, that s/he is the legitimate child of her/his parents or that s/he has been legitimated. If the declaration of parentage is granted, the birth can be re-registered.

However, objections raised in response to these proposals led the Commission to conclude that it was unacceptable to provide unmarried fathers automatically with such rights and that such a provision could operate to the detriment of the children concerned.

As a result, while biological fatherhood does not automatically bestow parental rights (see below), an unmarried father became entitled under the Family Law Reform Act 1987 to apply for a parental responsibility order (see Box page 37). The Act also extended the rights of biological fathers to enter their name as father on the register of births even without the consent of the mother, although they must have a court order to do so.

By granting the unmarried biological father almost the same rights as the married father, the Family Law Reform Act emphasised, for the first time this century, the importance of the genetic link between father and child. Historically, English common law has chosen only to recognise the relationship between a father and a legitimate child. The genetic link was a necessary condition for legal fatherhood, but not a sufficient one. However, the future importance in legislation of the genetic link is likely to be curtailed by the regulation of new techniques of assisted reproduction (Douglas and Lowe, 1993 and *Scientific advances in reproduction* page 36).

The Family Law Reform Act 1987 also set the rule that after 1988 no references to parents in legislation must be construed with regard to whether or not they were or have been married to each other. Again this reflected changes in attitudes to the stigmatisation of children on the basis of their parents' marital status.

The Children Act 1989 reflected this change in its discussion of parental responsibility and also enabled a putative father to acquire parental responsibility by agreement with the mother and to obtain contact orders if his child(ren) were in care. Further change may still be necessary since few unmarried cohabiting fathers seem to be aware of their rights and act to take them up (McRae, 1993).

When is the biological father not the legal father?

In law, a child's biological father is recognised as her/his legal father, with just three exceptions:

- when a married man rebuts the (automatic) presumption that he is the biological father of a child born to his wife and paternity is claimed by another man;
- when the child is born of artificial insemination or embryo donation to the wife, the child will be treated in law as the child of the husband if the mother is married (or of the male partner of the mother if she is unmarried), unless (a) it is proved that the husband or male partner did not consent to the treatment and (b) the marital presumption is rebutted;
- when the child is conceived using genetic material from a man who has already died.

Scientific advances in reproduction

Scientific advances in fertility treatment, including new techniques for treating infertility and experimenting with embryos, have prompted the need for regulatory legislation. The Human Fertilisation and Embryology Act 1990 regulates the creation of embryos outside the body, or the use of donated gametes, and makes it necessary for the provision of such services to the public to be licensed.

Where donated sperm is used for a woman in the course of 'licensed treatment services' provided for her and her partner together, her partner is treated as the father of the child. So an unmarried father can acquire the legal status of father of his partner's child even though he is not the genetic father. Furthermore, there is no requirement to show that the couple are cohabiting.

However, if a woman inseminates herself with semen obtained from a friend this does not have to be licensed, since services are not being offered to the public. If the woman is not married, the donor may be treated as the father since he is not protected from the legal consequences of his genetic link with the child by the rules governing statutory consents. By treating the donor as the father, the Act provides a disincentive to using unlicensed treatments and encourages licensed providers to consider the child's need for a social father.

In the case of a surrogacy agreement, the Act allows a married couple to apply for a parental order that the child be treated as theirs if one or both of them is a genetic parent of the child. This provision avoids the necessity for the couple to apply to adopt the child and the close scrutiny that it involves.

Parental responsibility

The concept of parental responsibility introduced by the Children Act 1989 embraces all the rights, duties, powers, responsibilities and authority which by law parents have to their children and their property. Parental responsibility includes the right to physical possession, the power to control education, to discipline, to administer property, to consent to medical treatment, to contact with the child and to represent the child in legal proceedings.

The introduction of parental responsibility has widened the range of people who may be entitled to some legal standing in relation to a child, with the proviso that parental rights yield to the child's rights to make her/his own decisions when s/he reaches 'sufficient understanding and intelligence' to be able to make up her/his own mind.

Do fathers automatically have parental responsibility?

If a child's mother and father were married to each other at the time of the birth,[1] they each have parental responsibility for that child, according to the Children Act 1989. Both parents also have parental responsibility automatically if:

- the marriage was void but either party reasonably believed it to be valid (Legitimacy Act 1976);
- the father and mother subsequently marry (Legitimacy Act 1976); and

- an adoption order is made, thus giving parental responsibility to the adoptive parents and cancelling that of the natural parents (see Box, page 38).

If the father is not married to the mother, only the mother automatically has parental responsibility. The father can obtain it by a parental responsibility order or a formal agreement with the mother (see below), or through a Section 8 residence order (see below page 39).

Acquiring parental responsibility

Parental responsibility order

An unmarried father can apply to the court for a parental responsibility order for a child. In deciding to make the order the court will treat the child's welfare as paramount but does not have to apply the statutory checklist of conditions to be fulfilled contained in s.1(3) of the Children Act 1989 (see section on Divorce). The order places the unmarried father in the same position as his married counterpart, that is he holds the parental rights and duties with the mother, except that the order can be brought to an end by an application to court.

The rights conferred by the order (that are additional to those the father already has as a 'parent') are not immediately enforceable. The order merely enables a father to apply to the court for the same orders as a married father (Dewar and Parker, 1992). If, for example, an unmarried father is in conflict with the mother over their child's medical treatment or schooling, he still has to apply to the court, although he would be on equal footing with the mother, since they would both have parental responsibility.

An application to bring a parental responsibility order to an end may only be made by an application to the court by a person with parental responsibility for the child or, with the leave of the court, by the child. In 1994, 3,885 parental responsibility orders were made (Lord Chancellor's Department, 1995). Information on the proportion of those made in favour of fathers is not collected.

Formal agreements

An agreement can be made by the parents of the child for the father to have parental responsibility. It will only be effective if it is in the prescribed form and registered with the High Court. Although registration is purely an administrative measure and does not involve any investigation into the child's welfare, the welfare principle does apply when the agreement is being terminated by a court order. In 1994, there were 4,522 agreements while births outside marriage numbered 215,000 (OPCS, 1995a).

Although an unmarried father does not automatically have parental responsibility, the law does recognise his relationship with the child. He can apply, therefore, for an order giving him parental responsibility without needing to ask the court for leave to do so.

An unmarried father also has some rights over the child's care, even without having parental responsibility. If the child is in care the local authority must allow him reasonable contact and has a qualified duty to ascertain the father's wishes and feelings.

If there is a dispute between parents, the welfare of the child is to be the court's paramount consideration in resolving the dispute. Unmarried fathers are also under a duty to maintain their child financially whether or not they have parental responsibility. However, in the case of the death of a child's mother, an unmarried father has to obtain a court order as his child's guardian before he can act as his or her legal representative.

Adoption

Adoption is the only way that a father's (or mother's*) parental responsibility can be removed, and is the means for an adoptive father (or mother*) to create a legal relationship with the child.

No adoption order can be made unless the father 'freely and with full understanding of what is involved' agrees unconditionally to the making of the order. If the father is married (or unmarried but has parental responsibility) his agreement is necessary and it must be dispensed with (see below) if it is not forthcoming.

The court can dispense with the agreement of the father at the adoption hearing, in six situations. The first three are the most often used. These are when the father:

- cannot be found or is incapable of giving agreement
- is withholding his agreement unreasonably
- has persistently failed without reasonable cause to discharge the obligations of a parent.

The remaining three situations relate to ill-treatment of the child and are rarely invoked in practice.

A father without parental responsibility may still have some involvement in the proceedings and an opportunity to prevent an adoption if the order for freeing the child for adoption is sought. At this stage the court must be satisfied that the unmarried father has no intention of applying for an order giving him parental responsibility, or that if he did, that it would be refused. The father who is liable to pay maintenance for the children also has a right to be heard in the adoption proceedings.

The adoptive father has parental responsibility for the child. He has all the rights and duties which a married father has in relation to his child and his property. The adoption order is irrevocable and the adoptive father's parental responsibility can only be removed by a further adoption. The order also extinguishes any other person's duty to pay child support for that child.

When a step-family is formed, the birth parent as well as the step-parent is legally obliged to become an adoptive parent. Agreement to the adoption is needed from the relinquishing parent if s/he has been married to one of the applicants or has parental responsibility. Step-family adoptions account for around a third of all adoptions.

* the provisions detailed in this box apply to both mothers and fathers.

A person does not cease to have parental responsibility because someone else acquires it. Parental responsibility can cease only on adoption (see Box). Each holder is entitled to exercise responsibility to the full, independently and without the need to consult any other holder. Their action must not, however, be incompatible with any court order or legal provision requiring the consent of all those holding parental responsibility (for example, removing the child from the United Kingdom for more than four weeks).

Section 8 orders

In addition to parental responsibility orders, Section 8 of the Children Act 1989 entitles an unmarried father to apply for an order relating to a range of issues concerning the care and residence of his children (see below).

Section 8 orders

There are four Section 8 orders:

1. *Residence orders* These settle who the child is to live with. They can be made in favour of two or more persons even if they do not live together. They replace the old custody orders.

2. *Contact orders* These require the person with whom the child lives to allow the child to visit, stay or have contact with a person named in the order. They replace the old access orders.

3. *Prohibited steps orders* These prevent any person from taking a specified step without the consent of the court.

4. *Specific issue orders* These give directions for the purposes of determining a specific question which has arisen, or may arise, in connection with any aspect of parental responsibility for a child.

A court can of its own accord make a Section 8 order in a father's favour. If a residence order is made in favour of an unmarried father, the court is obliged also to make a parental responsibility order in his favour. The courts take the view that contact with the non-residential parent is desirable and should be permitted unless there are convincing reasons for refusing it (Cretney and Mason, 1990). The fact that a child has had no relationship with a parent is not of itself a reason for refusing a contact order. A stepfather can also apply as of right for a Section 8 order if he has been married to the child's mother or has lived with the child for at least three years out of the last five.

Enforcement of Section 8 orders varies according to the court making the order. An order made by a Magistrates' Court can be enforced by a fine or commitment to custody for up to two months. The breach of an order made in the County or High Court can result in imprisonment for up to two years, sequestration of property and a fine.

When an order requiring a child to be handed over to another person is disobeyed, the court may authorise an officer of the court to enter premises, search for the child and deliver him to the person concerned. It not clear how effectively these orders are enforced.

Divorce

Both parents continue to have parental responsibility for their children if their marriage breaks down. They must file a detailed statement with the court of arrangements which have been made, or are proposed, for the upbringing and welfare of their children.

The court hearing the divorce case must consider whether it should use its powers under Section 8 of the Children Act 1989. Under the Act, court orders are to be made only if strictly necessary, and the welfare of the child is paramount. In practice this gives parents who co-operate with one another flexibility to make their own arrangements for the children and in most cases the courts will not make any orders about whom the children are to live with. Courts are likely to make Section 8 orders only when a conflict between parents cannot be resolved.

When the court does make an order with respect to the upbringing of a child, its paramount consideration must be the child's welfare. A checklist is contained in Section 1(3) of the Children Act 1989 to help the courts operate the welfare principle. Among the provisions to be considered are:

- the ascertainable wishes and feelings of the child concerned
- the child's physical, emotional and educational needs
- the likely effect of any change in circumstances
- how capable each parent is in meeting his or her needs.

In addition, as a general principle it is assumed that it is in children's best interests to have contact with adults who hold parental responsibility for them unless there is evidence to the contrary. The rights and suitability of the father are not directly taken into consideration by the court therefore, and are examined only in the context of the child's welfare.

The number of Section 8 orders made within divorce in 1992 to 1994 is shown in Table 3.1. No figures are collected for England and Wales on the number of residence orders made in favour of fathers, or made jointly.

Table 3.1   Section 8 orders made concerning children (England and Wales)

Year	Orders made within divorce			
	Contact	Prohibitive steps	Residence	Specific issue
1992	7,634	2,257	6,243	623
1993	11,799	2,500	8,611	658
1994	12,382	2,020	8,470	740

Source: Lord Chancellor's Department, 1995

Rights of fathers over their unborn children

The law and the courts have always denied the father of an unborn child any rights on the grounds that the child is part of the mother's body and that she should have exclusive rights over it.

The recent case of C v S confirms this: an Oxford student tried through the English courts to prevent his girlfriend from having an abortion. When the House of Lords did not prevent the abortion, he took the case to the European Court of Human Rights, arguing that this decision was in breach of the European Convention on Human Rights. The European Court confirmed the judgement of the House of Lords. (C v S (1987) 1 [AER] 1230 C A)

Financial responsibilities

The assessment and enforcement of maintenance (child support) payments for children is regulated by the Child Support Act 1991 (CSA) (see Chapter 6). This Act makes each parent of a 'qualifying' child for whom one or both parents is an 'absent parent' (i.e. non-resident), responsible for maintaining her or him and applies to the children of married, unmarried, separated and divorced parents alike. Similarly a father has to comply with the Act even if he is under 16 or was under 16 at the time of conception, although liability to pay is distinguished from ability to pay.

The father is also financially responsible in cases where his partner chose to have a child without informing him and he wanted her to have an abortion. In the case of artificial insemination (or embryo donation), for example, the partner will usually be recognised as the father and will be under an obligation to maintain the child (see *Scientific advances in reproduction* page 36). If the mother is neither married nor attached and confirmation of an anonymous donor (clinic, doctor and dates) is provided, the child will be recognised as having no known father. However, if the artificial insemination was informal and the father is known, he will be financially liable.

Under the Criminal Justice Act 1991, parents are responsible for any financial penalties imposed on their children aged under 16, unless that would be unreasonable. Where the young person is over 16, the duty on the court to order parents to pay is replaced by a power to decide whether so to order. In the same vein, young people aged 16 or 17 are also to be considered independent of their parents and responsible for their own actions, and it is their means rather than those of their parents which are to be taken into account.

The court is now under a duty to bind over, that is to subject to a legal obligation, the parents of a young offender if it is satisfied that this would prevent the young offender from committing further offences. If the court is not satisfied, it must give its reasons. The court can bind the parent over by a recognisance. This is a bond by which the parent engages before the court to take proper care of the offender and exercise control over her/him. The recognisance, for a sum of not more than £1,000, lasts three years, or until the offender is 18, whichever is the shorter period. If the parent does not consent to the recognisance and the court considers this unreasonable, the court can impose a fine of up to £1,000 on the parent.

International law

International law may also affect the rights and responsibilities of fathers, or have the potential to do so. The ratification of the Hague Convention on Civil Aspects of Child Abduction, for example, resulted in the passing of the Child Abduction and Custody Act 1985, Part I. This Act regulates the rights of parents whose child is wrongfully removed or detained in another state. International treaties guaranteeing human rights such as the European Convention on Human Rights and the UN Convention on the Rights of the Child also directly or indirectly define the rights and duties of fathers.

Summary

In the past 20 years the law relating to fatherhood has changed considerably. Both the Family Law Reform Act 1987 and the Children Act 1989, for example, linked parental responsibility to genetic fatherhood where once it was a child's status as legitimate that was critical to the legal basis of a father–child relationship. Moreover, even without the genetic link an unmarried man can attain the status of 'fatherhood' if sperm for a couple is donated and treatment is through a licensed provider.

Today, therefore, unmarried fathers are not entirely debarred from parental responsibility or the legal status of fatherhood although their parental rights in law fall short of those held by married fathers, nor are they acquired automatically. The marital status of a father continues to be important in bestowing legal fatherhood as of right. As cohabitation and extramarital child-bearing increase in popularity, more fathers are at some legal disadvantage, particularly since very few seem to be aware of the limitations by their non-married status (McRae, 1993).

Some inconsistencies are also evident in recent developments in the law relating to fatherhood. The rights and responsibilities of fatherhood in the Family Law Reform Act 1987, the Children Act 1989 and the Family Law Act 1996 centre unequivocally around the well-being of their children. By contrast, parental – frequently paternal – financial responsibility underlies those enshrined in the Child Support Act 1991 and is combined with parental responsibility for children's behaviour in the Criminal Justice Act of the same year. Arguably there is a contradiction between the financial responsibility for their children which the Child Support Act 1991 imposes irrespective of marital status and the fact that an unmarried father does not automatically acquire parental responsibility for his children but must apply for it. The law, moreover, makes a distinction between a father's obligation to make a financial contribution for his children's care and his right to have contact with them. Some fathers, on the other hand, see a very direct link between the two and legal developments may well be at odds with their perception of the natural order in these matters (Bradshaw, 1996; Clarke et al., 1996; Speak, 1996).

Notes

1. This includes marriage at the time of conception (or insemination), or births occurring very shortly after marriage or following a decree of divorce.

4 Fathers as breadwinners

The traditional division of family labour allocates fathers the role of breadwinner and mothers the care of home and family. This chapter looks at the current economic role of fathers in families and how this has changed, not least by comparison with the economic role now played by mothers. Attention is paid as well to the influence on fathers' economic role of changes in the distribution of male earnings, unemployment and age.

Fathers' employment

For most fathers, paid employment is a prerequisite for providing financially for their families. The employment rate for fathers has been consistently high – estimated at between 8 and 9 in 10 – since the beginning of the 1980s. Moreover, 9 out of 10 fathers in employment work full-time and they are more likely to be in employment than men without children (Table 4.1; Chapter 2; Harrop and Moss, 1994).

Table 4.1 **Employment status of fathers with children aged 1-10 years, 1993**

Country	Total	Full-time	Part-time	Unemployed	Economically inactive
	%	%	%	%	%
Belgium	92	91	1	4	4
Denmark	88	86	2	6	6
Germany	92	91	1	5	3
Greece	95	93	1	3	2
Spain	85	84	1	12	3
France	90	88	2	8	3
Ireland	81	78	2	13	7
Italy	93	91	1	4	3
Luxembourg	93	93	0	3	3
Netherlands	92	85	7	3	5
Portugal	95	93	1	3	3
Finland	80	77	3	15	6
Sweden	85	82	3	8	7
UK	84	82	2	11	5

Source: European Commission Network on Childcare (1996).

A Review of Services for Young Children.

None the less, this should not lead to complacency about fathers' employment. Comparative data shows (Table 4.1), for example, that the rate of employment (in 1993) for fathers with children under 11 years old in the UK was lower at 84% and their rate of unemployment was higher at 11% than in many other European countries (European Commission Network on Childcare, 1996). Overall unemployment has since increased in many of these countries and in some exceeds the UK rate of unemployment while previously having a lower rate (Department for Education and Employment, 1997).

By comparison with varying unemployment rates, throughout the European Union fathers' rates of part-time work in 1993 were consistent and low (Table 4.1). The United Kingdom is not unusual in having only 2% of employed fathers of young children working part-time (European Commission Network on Childcare, 1996). In addition, Joshi suggests that, according to data from the 1991 Census, there are as yet few families with dependent children in which fathers have taken the role of 'house husband' (Joshi, 1996).

Compared with fathers in two-parent families, lone fathers are less likely to be in employment (6 out of 10 compared with 9 out of 10 during 1986-90) (Haskey, 1993). Their lower employment rate reflects their child care responsibilities and is associated with a correspondingly higher rate of financial dependence on income support which has increased over time (Burghes, 1993; Department of Social Security, 1995a).

Hours of work

Men in the United Kingdom have among the longest average weekly hours of work of all men in Europe – more than 45 hours a week for full-time employees in 1995 – and these have been increasing (Eurostat, 1996; Watson, 1992; Social Trends, 1995 and 1996). Moreover, 4 in 10 male employees in the United Kingdom were working 46 hours or more a week in 1995. This was more than twice the proportion working these hours for men in any European Union country (Eurostat, 1996). Data now also shows that such long, and even longer, hours are common among fathers. Fathers of children under 11 years in the United Kingdom employed full-time were working 48 hours a week on average in 1993. This is four hours longer than the average for all fathers in Europe (European Commission Network on Childcare, 1996).

A substantial proportion of fathers, moreover, were working more than 50 hours a week by the end of the 1980s (Harrop and Moss, 1994). Similarly, Ferri and Smith (1996) found a fifth of the 33-year-old fathers in the NCDS 1991 working between 50 and 59 hours a week while weekly working hours for a further 10% exceeded 60 hours (Figure 4.1 and see endnote 2 to Chapter 1). The contrasting shorter working hours of mothers are also illustrated in Figure 4.1.

Being the sole earner in a family is associated with long hours at work for fathers (Brannen et al., 1995; Ferri and Smith, 1996). According to Brannen, first-time sole-earner fathers are, on average, at work for 55 hours a week during the first three years and their hours may increase during the early years of fatherhood (Brannen et al., 1995).

Long hours at work for sole-earner first-time fathers may reflect the (temporary) loss of the mothers' earnings at a time when family costs are rising.

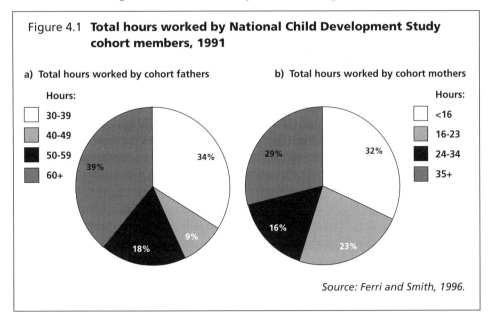

Figure 4.1 **Total hours worked by National Child Development Study cohort members, 1991**

a) Total hours worked by cohort fathers

b) Total hours worked by cohort mothers

Source: Ferri and Smith, 1996.

'Flexible' work

Alongside increasing hours of work, the structure of employment has been changing. Ten per cent of men and 15% of women employed full-time work some form of 'flexible' work pattern.[1] Similarly, working 'unsocial' hours – evenings, nights and weekends – is increasing (Hewitt, 1993). By 1991, Ferri and Smith (1996) found that more than a half of fathers (in the NCDS) were working outside 'normal hours' in both single-earner and dual-earner families. Two-thirds of the fathers were working in the evening and 6 in 10 at the weekends. Almost a third were working nights between 10pm and 4am and slightly more between 4am and 7am (Table 4.2).

Table 4.2 **Proportion of NCDS fathers working unsocial hours, 1991**

Cohort fathers	Dual-earner families with mother working		Single-earner families with father only working	All
	full-time	part-time		
	%	%	%	%
evenings (6pm-10pm)	67	63	67	65
nights (10pm-4am)	36	30	31	31
nights (4am-7am)	38	36	37	37
weekends	60	61	58	60
(approx n)	(318)	(846)	(843)	(2037)

Source: Ferri and Smith, 1996

The generic term 'flexible work' covers a number of working arrangements, not all of which make it easier, as the term may suggest they do, for fathers to combine work and family life, or mean that fathers are able to take time off when necessary to look after their children. 'Unsocial' working hours can also hinder joint family activities as fathers and mothers juggle work and child care and spend less time at home together with their children. Ferri and Smith (1996) found some evidence for reduced joint family activities for those working 'unsocial' hours, particularly in the evenings. But there was a more marked reduction in family activities for fathers who worked long hours, with a notable reduction in such activities where fathers worked more than 50 hours and an increase for those working less than 40 hours.

Working mothers: the rise of the dual-earner family

The employment of mothers in couples with dependent children has also been increasing – from just under a half (47%) in 1973 to 6 in 10 in 1995 (Office of Population Censuses and Surveys 1997). The rise in the employment of mothers is reflected in the increase in dual-earner families at the expense of the sole-earner father (Figure 4.2). Dual-earner families are now the norm among couples with children (Dex and Taylor, 1994; Office of Population Censuses and Surveys, 1997); in the 1995 General Household Survey both partners were working in 62% of married couples of working age with dependent children (Figure 4.3) (Office of Population Censuses and Surveys, 1997). The proportion of dual-earner couples increased with the age of the youngest child from just over a half (52%) for families with youngest child under 5 years to almost three-quarters (74%) where the youngest child was at least 10 years old (Office of Population Censuses and Surveys, 1997).

Figure 4.2 **Trends in employment of married couples with dependent children**

Source: General Household Survey, Office of Population Censuses and Surveys (1996)

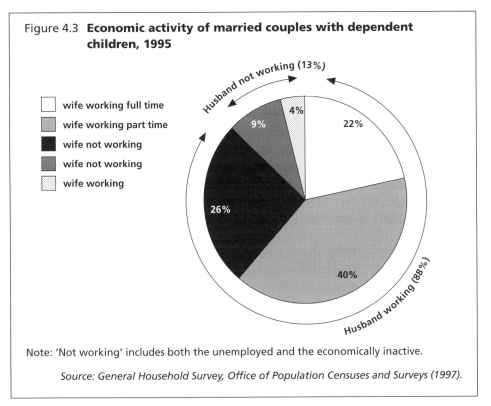

Figure 4.3 **Economic activity of married couples with dependent children, 1995**

Legend:
- wife working full time
- wife working part time
- wife not working
- wife not working
- wife working

Husband not working (13%)

Husband working (88%)

4%
9%
22%
26%
40%

Note: 'Not working' includes both the unemployed and the economically inactive.

Source: General Household Survey, Office of Population Censuses and Surveys (1997).

While mothers are increasingly likely to be in employment, part-time work still predominates. The economic activity of married couples with dependent children is shown in Table 4.3. Mothers with dependent children in employment whose husbands are also working are almost twice as likely to be working part-time as full-time (Office of Population Censuses and Surveys, 1997). Moreover, mothers as sole family earners are still a rarity at less than 5% of married couples with dependent children.

Table 4.3 **Economic activity of married couples with dependent children, 1995**

	Great Britain
	%
Two earners	62
- wife full-time	22
- wife part-time	40
Husband only working	26
Wife only working	4
No earner	9

Source: General Household Survey, Office of Population Censuses and Surveys (1997)

What effects have these developments had on the breadwinning role of fathers? Despite the growth in the employment of mothers, fathers are the sole breadwinner in a quarter of families with dependent children. If these sole-breadwinner fathers are combined with full-time working fathers whose wives work part-time, then fathers could be said to be the 'main breadwinner' in 6 out of 10 families with dependent children.[2]

Fathers as breadwinners

With few exceptions, it is through employment that fathers are able to be breadwinners for their families, even though employment is no guarantee of adequate financial provision for families, both because of the variation in the economic rewards of paid employment and because an equitable distribution of income within families cannot be assumed (Henwood *et al.*, 1987).

Despite these provisos, two-parent families are on average financially better-off either than families without a resident father (see Table 4.4) (Bradshaw and Millar, 1991; Brannen *et al.*, 1995; Burghes, 1995b; Hills, 1995; Office of Population Censuses and Surveys, 1996; Webb, 1994) or, self-evidently, where a resident father is unemployed (Child Poverty Action Group, 1995a; Goodman and Webb, 1994).

The distribution of income in lone-father families is more dispersed (see Table 4.4). In 1994, one-third of lone-father families had low gross weekly household incomes (of no more than £150 a week), while a further third had incomes of at least £350 a week. This reflects both their greater financial dependence on income support and their somewhat poorer occupational profile compared with married fathers. They are less likely, for example, to be in professional and managerial occupations and (like lone mothers) more likely to work in personal and service occupations (Haskey, 1993).

Table 4.4 Usual gross weekly household income by family type of families with dependent children (Great Britain, 1994)

Family type	Usual gross weekly household income						
	Up to £100	Over £100 up to £150	Over £150 up to £200	Over £200 up to £250	Over £250 up to £300	Over £300 up to £350	Over £350
	%	%	%	%	%	%	%
Married couple	4	6	6	7	7	8	62
Lone mother	47	20	10	5	5	5	8
Lone father	[27]	[9]	[9]	[7]	[5]	[7]	[36]

Note: Dependent children are persons under 16, or aged 16-18 and in full-time education. Numbers in brackets indicate a small base.

Source: General Household Survey 1994, Office of Population Censuses and Surveys (1996)

The influence of fathers' earnings on family incomes is seen clearly in Table 4.5. According to these General Household Survey figures (for 1990-92), fathers' earnings gave families an average weekly additional income of between £160 and £220 a week over mothers' earnings.

Table 4.5 **Current average net weekly earnings for mothers and couples, 1990-92**

	mothers	couples
	£	£
Family type:		
Single lone mother	87.4	-
Other lone mothers	102.0	-
Cohabiting couples	105.2	266.3
Married couples	100.1	320.8

Source: Burghes, 1995b

The decline of the male provider: fathers' and mothers' contributions to family incomes

Fathers are more likely now, of course, to share the economic role of breadwinning with their partners than they were in earlier decades. During the 10 years 1979-81–1989-91 the real earnings of both men and women increased. None the less, the contribution of male earnings to the increasing total family income of all couples fell from just under three-quarters (73%) to 60%, while over the same period the share of female earnings to total family income of all couples increased from 15% to one-fifth (Harkness *et al.*, 1995).[3] This increase in the contribution to family income of women in couples is accounted for by the combination of their increasing labour market participation rate over the period (from 55% to 71%) and the real growth in the earnings of those in work (by 92% compared with 23% for men) (Harkness *et al.*, 1995).

But within couple families the relative shares of family income contributed by men and women remained all but unchanged over the period; women working full-time on average consistently contributed just over 40% of family income and those working part-time around a fifth. By 1989-91, one in five women were contributing more than their partner to the family budgets; in 1979-81, only one woman in fifteen had done so (Harkness *et al.*, 1995).

As would be expected, the proportionate shares contributed by mothers and fathers to total family income are somewhat different from those of all men and all women. Fathers make a slightly higher contribution (by comparison with the average for all men in couples with and without children); mothers make a slightly lower contribution (by comparison with all women in couples with and without children).

None the less, differences between the shares of 'all men' and fathers and 'all women' and mothers to total family income are small and the change over time is in the same direction. Between 1979-81 and 1989-91 the share of total family income contributed by fathers fell from three-quarters to 65%; that of mothers increased from 10% to 16% (Harkness, 1996).[4]

A somewhat different picture is revealed for dual-earner couples with dependent children. By comparison with all families with children, the earnings contribution of mothers was and is higher (shifting from 22% to 24% between 1979-81 and 1989-91), while that of fathers was lower, but has declined less (from 71% to 67% over the same period) (Harkness, 1996).

'Work-poor' and 'work-rich': the shifting distribution of family incomes

Attention is frequently focused on the disparity in incomes between households whose members are or are not in employment – the 'work-rich' and 'work-poor' families (Social Security Committee, 1995a). Alongside this development, the rise in the dual-earner family is increasing the disparity of incomes within employed family households (Goodman and Webb, 1994; Gregg, 1995; Hills, 1995; Machin and Waldfogel, 1994). For example, as the BHPS shows, dual-earner households with children under 16 had higher average incomes in 1991 (at £2,393 a month) than those with a single earner – usually the father (at £1,692 a month) (Brannen *et al.*, 1995).

The rise in households with two earners in full-time well-paid employment in part explains the increasing inequality in household incomes; by contrast, the inequality between these better-off households and those headed by low-paid men would be even greater were it not for the financial contribution of their working wives (Machin and Waldfogel, 1994). The contribution to household income by these wives increased more during the 1980s than in earlier periods, when it was the wives of the well-paid whose employment most increased (Hills, 1995).

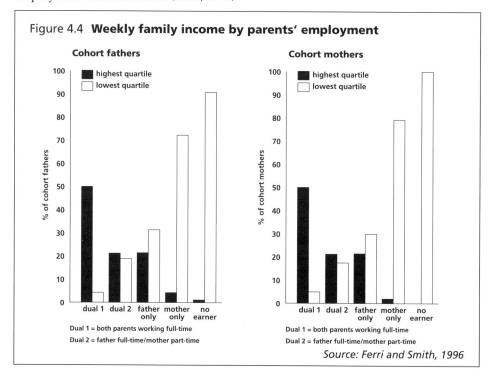

Figure 4.4 **Weekly family income by parents' employment**

Source: Ferri and Smith, 1996

A further element to this is revealed by Ferri's and Smith's (1996) analysis. Figure 4.4 shows that when both parents work full-time they are all but guaranteed a family income above the lowest quartile. On the other hand, dual-earner families with full-time fathers and part-time mothers are just as likely to be in the top as bottom income quartile, reflecting the range of male and female earnings these families command and the commonly more limited returns to part-time employment.

This supports recent analyses which show that the growth in women's labour force participation is in part a response to increasing inequality in the distribution of male earnings (Hills, 1995). Financial considerations figure high in women's reasons for working (Harkness *et al.*, 1995; Martin and Roberts 1984) and, in contrast to the earnings of men, those for women show relative gains in the past 20 years (Harkness *et al.*, 1995).

Unemployment

Just as the dual-earner family has become increasingly common, so too has the 'no-earner' family (Figure 4.2, p. 46). Recent shifts in demand have hit unskilled men and more recently those in white-collar occupations, increasing their risk of unemployment as well as low pay (Brannen *et al.*, 1995; Machin and Waldfogel, 1994).

While the increasing labour market participation of mothers in part wards off the consequences of the declining real earnings of men, it rarely does so – even in part – once he has lost his earnings altogether. The lower rate of employment among wives of unemployed than of employed husbands is well documented and remains unchanged. Likely explanations for unemployment among couples are the social security system's discouragement of the employment of the wives of men out of work and the likelihood that men and women with similar work backgrounds marry one another (Davies *et al.*, 1992). In families with dependent children, around a third of mothers with husbands who are unemployed or economically inactive work, compared with 7 in 10 of those with a working husband (Office of Population Censuses and Surveys, 1996; Figure 4.3, p. 47). 'No-earner' households have the lowest incomes of all (a result of their likely financial dependence on social security) and, as a result, rising unemployment is associated with increases in the number of families with children with low incomes (Brannen *et al.*, 1995; Child Poverty Action Group, 1995a; Goodman and Webb, 1994; Social Security Committee, 1995a).

Ferri and Smith found, moreover, that no-earner families were characterised by multiple disadvantages: 40% of the fathers had no formal educational qualifications; a third had semi- or unskilled jobs as their most recent occupation and more than 1 in 10 had four or more children (Ferri and Smith, 1996).

Young fathers, young families

A noticeable trend in recent years has been rising and high unemployment among young men (Allard, 1996; Trades Union Congress, 1996a). More specifically, the rate of unemployment among young fathers is considerably higher than it is for young men who do not have children. For example, almost a half of the 20 to 24-year-old fathers in the 1992 BHPS were unemployed. This was three times the rate for young men in this age group who were not fathers, many of whom would have been students (Clarke *et al.*, 1995).

In part this is a reflection of *"the decline in skilled trades occupations"* which *"has significantly reduced the role that such occupations played as 'entry' occupations for young males"* (Elias and Gregory, 1994). Moreover, wage rates of 'entry' jobs have fallen both relatively and absolutely over the past 20 years (Gregg and Wadsworth, 1996) and the gap in earnings commanded by those with and without educational qualifications has been growing, the more so for younger workers (Joseph Rowntree Foundation, 1995). These changes have had repercussions for young families. Kiernan suggests, for example, that while in the mid-1970s *"relatively full employment and the wider availability of manual and unskilled jobs made it easier for young people to marry and start a family within a few years of leaving school at the minimum age"*, the more predominantly service economy that has replaced it *"offers low wages to those without qualifications and training to compete for better-paid jobs"* (Kiernan, 1995b).

While the result has been, in part, a postponement of marriage and parenthood, men who do become fathers when they are young run greater risks of social and economic disadvantage and are likely themselves to have come from families which experienced financial hardship (Kiernan, 1995b). Young unemployed fathers lack the status that employment bestows and are unable to make financial provision for their children. Unemployment may also reduce the likelihood of young mothers and fathers forming residential parent partnerships (Burghes, 1995b).

Family breadwinning: whose responsibility?

The changes taking place in the employment of fathers and mothers and in the contribution they make to family incomes raise the issue of how fathers now regard their breadwinning role. According to the British Social Attitudes Survey, just over a half (53%) of British men and 42% of women agree that *"A husband's job is to earn money; a wife's job is to look after the home and family"* (Scott *et al.*, 1993).

Thus almost a half of British men do not support the traditional breadwinning model. Dench suggests that the role of primary economic breadwinner is not one that men willingly choose, but which they have thrust upon them. None the less, the imposition of that role is held to civilise men and relieve women of the burden of providing financially for themselves and their children (Dench, 1994).

Either way, for the foreseeable future, it would seem unlikely that available labour market opportunities will enable all fathers to provide as sole breadwinners for their families. Nor are women likely willingly to give up their place in the labour market faced with the limited returns from it available to some fathers as sole earners and a (perceived) high risk of family breakdown which may necessitate mothers' greater financial self-sufficiency.

Summary

Demographic, social, economic and legal changes in recent decades have made significant changes to the economic role of fathers. While employment rates for fathers are high, rates of unemployment among fathers are not insignificant and have serious financial implications for families. Lone fathers are less likely than fathers in couples to be in employment. The average working hours of fathers of young children are long and sole-earner fathers tend to work longer hours still. Working 'unsocial' hours – evenings, nights and weekends – has become commonplace.

Breadwinning is no longer the sole preserve of fathers. But while the dual-earner family has become the norm, mothers are still more likely to work part-time than full-time and in a quarter of economically active couples with dependent children the husband is the sole earner.

As the employment of women has increased, so too has their contribution to family incomes. Conversely, the contribution of male earnings has declined. None the less, fathers' earnings still account for the bulk of family income and mothers' earnings for a minority share.

Recent changes in Britain's occupational structure have reduced the employment opportunities for young men to support families that were available to them 20 years ago. By contrast, unemployment among young men has risen and it is higher still for young fathers, at the same time that entry wage rates have fallen both absolutely and relatively.

Notes

1. These flexible working patterns include flexible and annualized working hours, a four-and-a-half-day week and nine-day fortnight, term-time working and job sharing (*Social Trends*, 26, table 4.15. HMSO).

2. This may slightly overestimate fathers' breadwinning role because part-time employment among fathers is not taken into account. However, both Table 4.1 and 1991 Census data show a very low incidence of part-time working among fathers with dependent children. The 1991 Census showed less than 1% of couples with dependent children to include a man working part-time (Joshi, 1996).

3. This analysis uses General Household data for women aged 24-55 in cohabiting or married couples. Non-labour income makes up the residue of family income and increased over the period (1979-81 to 1989-91) from 12% to 18%.

4. This includes dual-earner, father-sole-earner, mother-sole-earner and no-earner families. The non-labour share of family income rose over the period and the increase was relatively greater for all couple families than for those with children. See also Note 3.

5 Fathers and family life

This chapter explores the role of fathers in daily family life; their share of the domestic chores and child care, and what fathers and children do together. It considers whether these have changed over time and how fathers feel about their contribution.

Comparisons of the 'social' contribution of fathers and mothers to family life has often, if implicitly, taken a gendered division of labour – fathers 'at work' and mothers 'at home' – as its benchmark. Today, the greater labour market participation of mothers and the rise of the dual-earner family need to be taken into account. There is as well substantial and increasing support for a more egalitarian division of household labour, although such attitudes are not universal, especially among older generations (Scott, 1990; Witherspoon, 1988).

Family life has been altered as well by family disruption and family reconstitution (Chapter 2) and 'not living together' affects contact between fathers and their children and what they do together. This issue is considered in the next chapter, while issues concerning lone fathers and stepfatherhood are touched on here.

A historical perspective on child care

Fathers are often assumed to have been until recently little involved in the care of their children (Parmenter, 1993). That they were involved, however, and sometimes considerably so, is also documented (Lummis, 1982; Newson and Newson, 1963; Wheelock, 1990). The Newsons' early 1960s study of the care of babies under a year old, for example, reported a half of the fathers to be 'highly participant' in their care (even though playing with their children was not defined as 'care') (Newson and Newson, 1963).

Since there is little, if any, representative quantitative data on fathering, however, it is difficult to gauge how widespread was such involvement of fathers in their children's care. Indeed, Lummis suggests that *"Most evidence for the role of the father in history is little more than anecdotal … usually a surface response … to what is believed to be the social norm"* (Lummis, 1982).

Caring for their children today

Because of shifts in expectations of fatherhood, fathers may have been reluctant in the past to admit to too much involvement in child care and domestic activities; now they may be reluctant to admit too little. It may be difficult, as a result, to judge whether and in what ways fatherhood has changed. Lewis (1995a), for example, argues that *"there is a striking similarity between parental accounts of fatherhood in the 1950s with those of the 1980s"*. While fathers now may feel that they are more involved with their young children than were their own fathers, the evidence may not yet show that they are.

Undoubtedly many fathers are involved in the care of their children and their involvement has increased (Martin and Roberts, 1984; Meltzer, 1994). A 1990 survey, for example, reported that a fifth of pre-school-age children were regularly cared for by their fathers when their mothers were absent (Meltzer, 1994). Similarly, more than a third of the 33-year-old mothers in the 1991 NCDS reported that their husbands provided child care (Ferri and Smith, 1996 see endnote 2 to Chapter 1, p. 14).

Gershuny suggests that both men and women are spending more time on child care than they were 30 years ago. Indeed, time spent on child care increased more for men (fourfold) than for women (two-and-a-half times) between 1961 and 1995. Women, however, were still spending almost one and three-quarters as much time as men on child care by the end of the period (Gershuny, 1996). Ringen and Halpin (1995) also report both that the gap between the time wives and husbands spend on child care has narrowed and that the extent of women's time greatly exceeds that of their partners.

On the other hand there is also evidence for the sharing of child care between husbands and wives (Ferri and Smith, 1996; Martin and Roberts, 1984). Thus in the 1980 Women and Employment survey (Martin and Roberts, 1984) a half of mothers and 44% of fathers said child care was shared equally, while Ferri and Smith (1996) report almost 45% of NCDS 1991 cohort mothers and 50% of cohort fathers claiming the responsibility for child care was shared.

Both Martin and Roberts (1984) and Ferri and Smith (1996) (Table 5.1) also found that fathers become more involved in the care of their children as mothers' participation in the labour market increases and both mothers and fathers report care to be more likely to be shared between them (even if fathers report more shared care than do mothers). None the less, Ferri and Smith (1996) report that even in families with the most egalitarian child-care arrangements – those in which both parents work full-time – a quarter of the fathers report that mothers are still mainly responsible for child care, while a third of the mothers report being mostly responsible for it.

When mothers work part-time they are more likely than are full-time working mothers to take the main responsibility for their children, and a smaller proportion of husbands and wives report that they share looking after their children between them (Ferri and Smith, 1996). Sole-earner fathers provided the least care for their children (Table 5.1) and fathers who worked long hours were found to spend less time caring for their children (data not shown) (Ferri and Smith, 1996).

Ferri and Smith also compared how fathers' involvement with their children had changed between the 1965 and 1991 sweeps of the NCDS (although the questions asked were not identical at the two sweeps). In 1965, 6 out of 10 fathers were described as 'playing an equal part' in managing their children, while in 1991 a half of fathers were said to 'share equally' in the general care of their children. Ferri and Smith (1996) suggest that *"This finding puts in some perspective any claim that there has been a radical shift in the parenting roles of fathers over the past generation"*.

Table 5.1 'Who is normally responsible for generally being with and looking after children', NCDS 1991

	cohort fathers			
	dual-earner		single-earner	
	wife f/t	wife p/t	wife home	wife works
	%	%	%	%
mostly father	2	1	<1	16
mostly wife	24	42	68	21
shared equally	72	57	32	61
someone else	2	-	<1	2
Total	100	100	100	100
(N)	(397)	(993)	(1008)	(44)

	cohort mothers			
	dual-earner		single-earner	
	mother f/t	mother p/t	mother home	mother works
	%	%	%	%
mostly husband	1	<1	-	9
mostly mother	32	52	72	26
shared equally	66	48	28	64
someone else	1	-	-	1
Total	100	100	100	100
(N)	(532)	(1261)	(953)	(66)

Source: Ferri and Smith, (1996)

Moreover, whatever increase there has been in the caring role of fathers, mothers still remain responsible for organising this care (Brannen *et al.*, 1995; Cappuccini and Cochrane, 1996; Gershuny, 1995a; Jackson, 1987; Lamb, 1995).

A number of studies have looked at the division of parental responsibility for particular aspects of child care, such as the teaching of good behaviour or discipline and the care of sick children (Kiernan, 1992a; Ferri and Smith, 1996; Martin and Roberts, 1984; Witherspoon, 1988).

Compared with general child care, 'teaching good behaviour' or 'discipline' both was and is much more likely to be shared equally between parents – in 8 out of 10 cases. More than 8 out of 10 cohort fathers and cohort mothers in the 1991 NCDS report sharing equally the 'teaching of good behaviour' (Ferri and Smith, 1996). The nationally representative British Social Attitudes Surveys reported parents in three-quarters of households to share teaching children discipline (in 1991) and that this differed little by the mothers' employment position (Kiernan, 1992a).

By contrast, caring for sick children is less likely to be shared equally, and falls to mothers rather than fathers (Ferri and Smith, 1996; Kiernan, 1992a; Martin and Roberts,

1984; Witherspoon, 1988). Both the 1991 British Social Attitudes Survey and the 1991 NCDS reported that around a third of couples shared equally caring for sick children, while mothers were mainly responsible in the remainder of cases. Despite the predominance of mother care for sick children, the British Social Attitudes Survey reports a marked increase in men's care for sick children since 1987 (Kiernan, 1992a).

What do fathers and children do together?

Where fathers are involved in the care of their children, studies repeatedly report that it is with the more pleasurable and leisure aspects of child care; the 'rough and tumble' play between fathers and children in early childhood and sports activities as they get older (Brannen et al., 1995; National Opinion Poll, 1995). On the other hand, Lewis has pointed out that the stereotyping of fathers as playing more with their children than do mothers is not always borne out by the evidence. Indeed, the evidence may be fitted to match the preconception (Lewis, 1982). Similarly, Ferri and Smith (1996) comment that asking NCDS mothers about fathers' outdoor activities with their children is "reinforcing somewhat the stereotypical view of the paternal role". None the less, the 1991 NCDS did find that the majority of fathers played with their children outdoors at least once a week. They were slightly more likely to do so with sons than with daughters, and with all children more so when both parents worked full-time but with a reduced likelihood if they worked long hours themselves.

The 600 East London 14-year-olds in O'Brien's and Jones' (1996) study reported spending four-and-a-half hours on a weekday with their fathers (that is 'being in the presence of' rather than necessarily engaging 'one-to-one'). Just four activities – watching TV, talking generally, talking about education and work, and doing 'nothing' – accounted for three-quarters of this time together (and the same was true for their mothers), with approximately equal proportions allocated to each activity. Time together increased by three hours at the weekend, boys spending more time than girls with their fathers. Indeed, O'Brien and Jones (1996) point out that weekends and holidays are times when fathers and their children may 'catch up' with time together, although this may be difficult for fathers who have become marginal to daily family life or who work at the weekends. Activities on Saturdays were oriented around shopping while leisure activities predominated on Sundays.

While sons are more likely than daughters to turn to their fathers for advice (O'Brien and Jones, 1996), both girls and boys are more likely to turn to their mothers (O'Brien and Jones, 1996; Ghate and Daniels, 1997). Young people also report somewhat more positive feelings about communication with their mothers (67%) than with their fathers (57%) (Catan, Dennison and Coleman, 1997). For a quarter, however, of the young people in O'Brien and Jones' (1996) study, their father was their favourite adult and the person they would turn to first with worries about money, their mothers and sport. In general the studies also reveal the importance young people attach to their fathers, to their 'being there' and to spending time together (O'Brien and Jones, 1996; Ghate and Daniels, 1997).

Evidence about the time fathers and children spend together is limited and not necessarily nationally representative. In addition to the reports from O'Brien and Jones (above), two-thirds of 14,000 self-selecting respondents to a survey by Sainsbury's in 1994 said that their children spent between one and three hours with their fathers every day (Sainsbury, 1994). By contrast, the 200 fathers in a 1995 National Opinion Poll survey reported spending five minutes or less on an average weekday with their children on a one-to-one basis (National Opinion Poll, 1995). Clearly, neither the samples nor the questions asked are comparable.

The involvement of fathers with their children can be approached by looking at what families do together. Information from the NCDS found families to be regularly engaged in joint activities. For example, almost two-thirds of families ate together at least once a day; more than 9 in 10 spent at least one evening a week together, more than 4 in 10 families went shopping together at least once a week, a quarter went out together at least once a week, and half visited friends or relatives at least once a week (Ferri and Smith, 1996). Family activities were less likely when fathers worked long hours. On the other hand, families in which fathers who were highly involved in the care of their children were those which did more activities together. Ferri and Smith (1996) conclude that this points to *"a group of relatively 'family oriented' fathers, who shared with mothers the responsibility for the care and upbringing of their children, and who also participated in a range of activities involving all members of the family"*.

The effect of family structure

What fathers and their children do together – as well as how much time they spend together – is increasingly affected by family structure. More research data is available for its effects on what fathers and children do together in the United States (not reported here) than in Britain (Cooksey and Fondell, 1996). Contact between non-resident fathers and their children is discussed in Chapter 6.

In contrast to fathers in two-parent families, lone fathers have day-to-day responsibility for their children (as well as the households chores). Hipgrave (1982) has argued that while there is *"no evidence that lone fathers cannot plan and organise a healthy developmental environment for their children ... there is a good deal of evidence that we, the community, make it extremely hard for them to do so"*. It is not known whether the current view that fathers should be more involved in caring and nurturing their children extends to allowing that today they are competent as lone parents.

The position of stepfathers is different again. Relationships with stepchildren are not uncommonly more problematic and what they do with their stepchildren and how much time they spend with them may be affected by this. Stepfathers may encounter reluctance on the part of their stepchildren in their attempts to establish good relationships with them (Booth and Dunn, 1994). None the less, in their study of fathers becoming stepfathers Burgoyne and Clark (1982) found the stepfathers *"frequently appeared highly reflective and self-conscious about relationships with their stepchildren ... being able to share the responsibilities and activities of child care more fully in a second marriage were frequent themes when our respondents compared past and present partners"*.

The domestic domain and household chores

As is so often the case, published studies do not always distinguish men who are fathers from those who are not. Data on the domestic division of labour for men suggests that they do take a share of the domestic chores, more than they once did, while women may be doing less than formerly, if only marginally so (Brannen *et al.*, 1995; Gershuny, 1995a; Gershuny and Robinson, 1988; Kiernan, 1992a; Ringen and Halpin, 1995). The decline in women's domestic activity reflects their increasing time in paid employment. In contrast *"men have increased their average hours of domestic work from low to less low levels, partially substituting for their wives"* (Joshi, 1996).

None the less, women still shoulder the lion's share of the domestic tasks – by two-thirds to men's one-third (two hours a day compared with one) according to Gershuny (1996) for the 'core domestic activities' of cooking, cleaning and laundry – and the gender stereotyping of these tasks continues (Brannen *et al.*, 1995; Gershuny, 1995a and 1996; *Social Trends*, 1995). On the other hand, at around three-quarters of an hour, men spend twice as much time as women a day on 'other domestic work' ('odd jobs' and gardening, for example) (Gershuny, 1996).

Women's participation in the labour market influences the distribution of the domestic chores. Couples who both work full-time are more likely to share their domestic duties. Despite this, two-thirds of women working full-time retain responsibility for them (Kiernan, 1992a). Tyrell reports, moreover, that the shorter working hours of women (than men) in full-time employment are more than matched by their 'non-discretionary' household chores (Tyrell, 1995). Women who work part-time ar e mostly responsible for the household chores. The proportion who are 'mainly responsible' for them is very little different to that of women who are not in work (Ferri and Smith, 1996; Kiernan, 1992a).

As far as the distribution of household chores among parents is concerned, fathers with young children are more likely than men in general to do household chores, although the overall distribution remains less than equal between partners (Witherspoon, 1985). Ferri and Smith (1996) analysed the reports, given by both fathers and mothers in the 1991 NCDS, of the organisation of domestic chores (shopping, cleaning, laundry, household repairs/DIY and family finances). According to fathers, the organisation of the domestic chores is most 'egalitarian' when both parents worked full-time (Table 5.2). Apart from laundry, which overwhelmingly falls to mothers, chores are shared equally in between a quarter and 40% of households. None the less, full-time working mothers were overwhelmingly responsible for the cooking, cleaning and laundry (Ferri and Smith, 1996). Mothers working part-time differed little in their responsibilities from mothers at home, and in every case these exceeded those of mothers working full-time. Sole-earner fathers were little involved in the domestic chores (laundry, cooking and cleaning) but three-quarters of all fathers were responsible for the household repairs and DIY. Responsibility for family finances was more varied than was the case for other household chores.

Table 5.2 **Fathers' responsibility for domestic chores**

Cohort father	dual worker		single worker	
	wife f/t	wife p/t	wife works	wife home
	%	%	%	%
Preparing/cooking main meal				
I do most	11	3	28	2
wife does most	62	82	49	88
shared equally	27	15	23	10
Shopping				
I do most	9	5	33	6
wife does most	51	67	49	66
shared equally	40	28	18	28
Cleaning				
I do most	2	1	17	1
wife does most	63	83	58	88
shared equally	35	16	25	11
Laundry				
I do most	2	1	15	1
wife does most	83	93	72	94
shared equally	15	6	13	5
Household repairs/DIY				
I do most	72	79	76	77
wife does most	2	3	5	5
shared equally	26	18	19	19
Household money/paying bills				
I do most	33	28	32	43
wife does most	37	45	50	34
shared equally	30	27	18	23

Note: Cohort fathers report of their responsibility for domestic chores.

Source: Ferri and Smith (1996). Unpublished tables 3.15-3.20 available from authors.

Unemployed fathers

The data in Table 5.2 also reveals the division of responsibility for domestic chores when the mother is the sole earner. Under these circumstances fathers report a marked increase in the extent to which they do most of the chores. However, mothers and fathers do not see entirely eye-to-eye about this division of labour. According to the sole-earner mothers, they remain mainly responsible for cooking, cleaning, shopping and laundry (data not shown in table). None the less, even according to the fathers' reports, only a minority of fathers become solely responsible for the core domestic chores while a half or more of the sole working wives still do the greater share of them (Ferri and Smith, 1996).

A similar picture emerges with regard to the general care of the children: fathers with sole-earner wives are more likely (at 16%) to report being normally responsible for looking after their children than other fathers (Table 5.1, page 57). The proportion reporting sharing responsibility for children's care is also greater (at 6 in 10) than for those with wives who do not work or who work part-time. Men's role as the main care provider increased in proportion to the mother's hours at work, and fathers became the major carer when their wives worked more than 35 hours (data not shown).

Tyrell has reported similarly from the Henley Time Use Survey that fathers who have working wives, but who are not themselves in employment, do not take over the major responsibility for child care or for the domestic chores from their wives. Rather shared care is the most common arrangement (Tyrell, 1995).

Activities and attitudes compared

What fathers do in the home and with their children may not, of course, be the same as what they would like to do. Indeed, there are likely to be discrepancies between their attitudes and their activities. Overall there is much greater and increasing attitudinal support over time for the equal sharing of household tasks than in practice takes place (Ferri and Smith, 1996; Kiernan, 1992a; *Social Trends*, 1995). Similar discrepancies between attitudes and activities are replicated throughout Europe (Commission of the European Community, 1991 and 1993). The gap between what fathers do and what they would like to do reflects the constraints of employment and/or other cultural, financial, institutional and structural factors. Fathers' expressed attitudes may also reflect their perception of what is socially acceptable – namely more rather than less fathering – rather than their own desire to be such a father. On the other hand, van Dongen suggests that fathers may be constrained by maternal attitudes, sensing *"the point at which their 'help' becomes trespassing"* (van Dongen, 1995) on the mother's domain.

Within parenting roles, parents' attitudes still seem to support a gender division of care and activities. In *The Europeans and the family* the Commission of the European Community (1993) report that in the United Kingdom playing sport with the children and giving them pocket-money were more likely to be thought of as tasks for fathers, while the care needs of children were more for mothers.

The effect of long and unsocial working hours may limit fathers' involvement in family life. It should not, however, be taken as necessarily implying a lack of care, but rather the nature of it (Lewis, 1995a). Fathers may care *about* and provide economically for their families even if they care *for* them to a more limited extent. This way of caring may be less ideologically acceptable today that it was once. Indeed, O'Brien (1982) reports that the work and home lives of fathers in professional and intermediate occupations conflicted because they were unable to share the domestic tasks as they thought they should. On the other hand, the conflict for fathers in working-class occupations was the reverse. They tended to be more involved in domestic tasks and child care than they felt they should be. O'Brien suggests that this reflects *"... the underlying belief that they were making a positive and valued contribution to the family through their work*

... their work role was their family role and so there was little perceived conflict between the two" (O'Brien, 1982). Cappuccini and Cochrane (1996) similarly report that while first-time fathers may think of their children as more important than their work, in practice the importance of work increases because of their financial responsibility for their children.

An alternative explanation is that fathers' long hours at work reflect their reluctance to take on more domestic tasks and child-related activities (Pleck, 1986). Indeed, dissatisfaction among fathers in the 1991 NCDS was greatest where they both worked very long hours and were involved with the care and behaviour of their children (Ferri and Smith, 1996). On the other hand, cultural and institutional constraints may militate against fathers who wish to reduce their hours of work, particularly where this is for family reasons. A survey of 106 fathers working reduced and flexible hours found that those who were doing so for child care reasons were considered to be challenging gender expectations; employers were less understanding of their work–family conflicts than of those faced by mothers (Collins and Walton, 1995).

Summary

It may be a popular misconception that fathers were not historically involved with their children and that such involvement is a purely modern phenomenon. There is too little reliable quantitative data by which to judge the distant past or the shift between then and now. As far as fathers' activities with their children are concerned, it has been commonly assumed that they are much more likely to engage in leisure activities than basic caring responsibilities. Here again the evidence is limited and may not be entirely reliable, too readily reflecting what it is thought appropriate for fathers to do with their children rather than what they actually do.

In more recent decades time-use studies do suggest fathers spend more time caring for their children, that the amount of time caring for children has increased more for men than for women and that the gap between mothers and fathers spent in child care has narrowed as a result. Mothers, none the less, still spend more time than fathers looking after their children and mothers remain largely responsible for organising their children's care. Fathers' contribution to the care of their children diminishes as their hours of work increase. Mothers still remain responsible as well for most household chores (apart from repairs and DIY) even in the most egalitarian of households, those in which both parents are working full-time. Ferri and Smith (1996) concluded that, while *"fathers' employment situation set the framework for their domestic contribution"*, for mothers *"family life and its related responsibilities were decisive factors influencing their involvement in the labour force"*.

Overall there is more support for greater equality in the sharing of household tasks than in practice takes place (Witherspoon, 1985, 1988; Kiernan, 1992a). Indeed Kiernan (1992a) points out that practice has failed to keep pace with increasingly egalitarian attitudes and the gap between the two has widened over time.

6 Non-resident fathers

By the beginning of the 1990s, between 1 in 6 and 1 in 7 fathers were not living with any of their biological children (Ferri, 1994; Chapter 2). The debate about fatherhood frequently treats fathers' physical and psychological presence and absence as synonymous. While fathers who do not live with their children are taken to be in every sense absent from and unavailable to them, resident fathers are assumed to be ever-present and always available. But neither is straightforwardly the case. While it may be more likely and easier for resident fathers to be physically and emotionally available to their children this does not mean that they always are so. Nor are non-resident fathers never present in their children's lives or entirely unavailable to them, even though it may be more difficult for them to be involved and less likely that they will be (Kraemer, 1995a; O'Brien and Jones, 1996).

To take account of this complexity, the terms 'resident' and 'non-resident', when used here, describe whether or not fathers live with their children and the terms 'absent' and 'present' whether fathers have contact with and are involved in their children's lives. (This does not entirely accord with common or official usage.)

The focus of this chapter, however, is on non-residential fatherhood and its implications for children. It explores the contact non-residential fathers have with their children, what influences contact, children's development and outcomes, and non-residential fathers' financial support for their children. The issue and consequences of resident fathers who are absent or little involved in their children's lives are beyond its scope. The chapter, in this respect, mirrors the recent policy debate about the role of fathers which has concentrated on non-residential fatherhood and its consequences. The lack of focus on the consequences of, for example, long working hours on the involvement of resident fathers in the lives of their children will need to be addressed.

Contact between fathers and their children

There is, clearly, likely to be less contact between fathers and their children when they do not live in the same household and this contact may diminish with time (Bradshaw and Millar, 1991; Clarke, 1997; Simpson et al., 1995). A number of datasets have been used to estimate the extent of contact with the children. According to the 1991 NCDS survey, for example, 7 in 10 fathers who do not live with their children none the less have contact with them (Clarke, 1997) and all children living apart from their father had, on average, lived with their fathers for about a half of their lives (Clarke et al., 1997). Three-quarters of the 90 divorced fathers in Relate's small-scale study also report seeing their children from whom they are living apart (Simpson *et al.*, 1995). Of the 600 non-resident fathers in the 1996 survey by Bradshaw and colleagues (1997) 80% had seen their children within the last year.

Until now, estimating contact has depended on reports from resident lone mothers and much lower levels of continuing contact between non-resident fathers and children were found. Bradshaw's and Millar's (1991) study of lone parents in the United Kingdom, for example, found that just over 4 in 10 non-resident parents (mothers and fathers) no longer had contact with their children. Lack of contact had increased over time (as measured by the duration of the lone parenthood of the partner from whom the non-resident parent was living apart). While 60% of non-resident parents were still in contact with their children after three years, this fell to just over 40% after 10 years (Bradshaw and Millar, 1991). A lack of consistency in the results between these surveys of lone mothers and those of non-resident fathers is likely to reflect differing sample characteristics.[1]

Maintaining contact and types of contact

Limited and declining contact over time may reflect not fathers' lack of interest in maintaining a relationship with their children, but the difficulties – whether social, financial, geographical and/or emotional – of doing so (Simpson *et al.*, 1995; O'Brien and Jones, 1996). The complexities and difficulties of post-divorce relationships between ex-spouses as well as post-divorce parenting should not be underestimated.

Moreover, there are a number of ways in which non-resident fathers can make themselves 'available' to their children. Indeed, Simpson *et al.* (1995) report non-resident fathers to feel that the term 'absent' is derisory and that 'being there' – if in other ways – is the most important thing that they can do for their children. Practical examples include helping with homework, attending school parents' evenings, taking to and from school, and elsewhere, and offering to provide an alternative home should it be needed (Bradshaw *et al.*, 1997; Simpson *et al.*, 1995). As O'Brien comments, both close and distant fathering are now taking place and different models of fathering are being negotiated (O'Brien, 1995).

While some fathers may not want to establish or maintain a relationship with their children, diminution in contact over time may also reflect children's increasing independence in adolescence. In their 1996 nationwide study of four thousand teenagers (12-19), Catan, Dennison and Coleman (1997) found communication was worst between young people and non-resident fathers. Failing communication was often frustrating and painful for the teenagers, while where it was successful, the researchers found it to be *"clearly central in the lives of teenage sons and daughters, providing positive role models of both relationships and communication"*.

It is sometimes suggested that fathers are less likely to live apart from sons than from daughters and more likely to remain in contact with their sons when they do (Mott, 1994; Smith and Morgan, 1994), but evidence on both points is limited as far as Britain is concerned. According to the BHPS 1992, fathers are in fact no more likely to live apart from their daughters than from their sons (see Chapter 2). By contrast, the

Relate study (Simpson *et al.*, 1995) reports that *"fathers were three times as likely to have lost contact with their children if those children were all daughters than if they were boys"*. This may suggest that gender is a relevant factor in continuing contact between fathers and their children and warrants further investigation.

At the other end of the spectrum are non-resident father–child relationships in which contact is frequent. Of all the non-resident fathers in the surveys (including those who did and did not see their children) Bradshaw and colleagues (1997) report that almost a half (47%) see their children at least once a week, as do almost 4 in 10 (37.8%) of those in the Relate qualitative investigation (Simpson *et al.*, 1995). Almost a half of the non-resident parents in Bradshaw's and Millar's study (1991) who were reported to have contact with their children saw them at least weekly. Fathers may want to spend more time than they do with their children, especially where contact is infrequent (Bradshaw *et al.*, 1997; Simpson *et al.*, 1995).

What influences contact with children?

Evidence suggests that contact is more likely between separated and divorced non-resident fathers and their children than it is for never-married fathers (Bradshaw *et al.*, 1997; Bradshaw and Millar, 1991; Seltzer, 1995). Among never-married fathers this may reflect the lack of an established long-term relationship with the child's mother. As the resident parent, mothers are likely to play a mediating role between non-resident fathers and their children, not only providing information about the child's development but also acting as a 'gate-keeper'.

Maintaining contact with children requires a co-operative parenting relationship between resident and non-resident parents such that arrangements can be made about when, where and for how much time non-resident fathers and their children will be together. Parental relationships before divorce thus may influence post-divorce relationships between fathers and their children, but they do not do so invariably. In the Relate study, fathers no longer in contact with their children were likely to have experienced a further deterioration over time in their relationship with their ex-partners (Simpson *et al.*, 1995). Fathers who had good parenting relationships started out with the most friendly relationships with their ex-partner and these had improved over time. None the less, a half of the fathers who had good communicative relationships with their ex-partner about their children did not have friendly personal relationships with them, suggesting *"that while continuing friendship may make communication easier it can continue where relationships are in other senses distant"* (Simpson *et al.*, 1995).

Evidence on the relationship between fathers' involvement with their children before and after divorce is not clear-cut. While some research has found a positive relationship between the two – fathers being involved with their children after divorce if they have been before the divorce – others report contrary evidence: fathers establishing a more active relationship with their children after the divorce than they had before it (Lewis, 1993 and 1995b; Seltzer, 1995; Simpson *et al.*, 1995).

Clearly, relationships can go either way, with many factors other than the prior father–child relationship influential or determinant. Not all fathers are able to negotiate a new relationship with their children independent of that mediated through the mother before the divorce. They may never have had sole care of their children, or not for extended periods. They may know too little about what their children can do or what they need to do with them (Simpson *et al.*, 1995). For other fathers, on the other hand, the separation allows them to *"discover the novelty of direct contact with their children, without mother as intermediary"* (Kraemer, 1995a) and get to know their children at some remove from a conflict-ridden parental relationship.

Material factors often play a part as well. Fathers with adequate income, housing and transport are more able and more likely to be in contact with their children, while the lack of these resources may diminish other fathers' ability to do so. A low income – and in some cases payment of child support itself – may restrict activities and hamper contact and non-resident fathers may not be able to keep in touch with their children (Bradshaw *et al.*, 1997, Clarke *et al.*, 1996; Simpson *et al.*, 1995). Non-resident fathers are more likely to be unemployed (by comparison with men of the same age in the general population) or employed in lower-paying occupations (partly explained by their younger age profile) (Burghes, 1991). In February 1997, a third of the non-resident parents assessed for child support by the Child Support Agency were in receipt of Income Support (Department of Social Security, 1997).

Non-resident fathers are not a priority for local authority housing and as they are treated similarly to single people may not be allocated accommodation sufficient for their children either to visit or to stay overnight. This is a particular problem when non-resident fathers and children become geographically distant. Indeed, contact between non-resident fathers and their children is less likely the greater the geographical distance between them (Bradshaw *et al.*, 1997). While most non-resident fathers and their children live close to one another, a minority are geographically distant. A half of non-resident parents assessed for maintenance by the Child Support Agency live less than 5km apart from one another, 1 in 7 live at 50km distance or more (Department of Social Security, 1997). Social and financial circumstances may thus further constrain contact between fathers and children who live apart; what time fathers and their children have together, what they are able to do together and where, being limited by how far they live from one another and the father's housing and income. Such difficulties may be particularly acute for young first-time fathers.

Emotional costs too may be a factor in failing or limited contact. Efforts to maintain contact 'in a hostile climate' – when the relationship between estranged parents is poor – may prove too demanding emotionally not only for fathers but, as they see it, for their children and new partners (if any) (Seltzer, 1995; Simpson *et al.*, 1995). But they may not willingly give up contact and see doing so as a temporary *"sacrifice aimed at ameliorating suffering all round"* (Simpson *et al.*, 1995). Fathers who maintain contact with their children may also do so at a cost to other aspects of their lives. The Relate study found these fathers had more personal and social problems and more difficulty in forming new relationships (Simpson *et al.*, 1995).

Fathers and children's development

The 1990s have witnessed heightened concern and public debate about the effects on children of non-residential fatherhood: the absence of fathers from children's lives and their consequence for children's development. These anxieties are not new, however, and it is beyond the scope of this chapter to review the extensive and complex debate, particularly in the psychological literature, about the relationship between fathers and children's development.

While recent research on the consequences of father non-residence and absence stems from anxieties about rising divorce rates in the 1960s, earlier concerns can be traced back to the Second World War, when the fathers of many children were away for prolonged periods and some children experienced bereavement. At this time it was feared that the sex role development of boys and their masculinity was being put at risk by their father's absence.

As far as the development of masculinity in boys is concerned, researchers report surprise at not finding a (direct) correlation with the amount of time boys spent with their fathers: boys who spent more time with their fathers were neither more likely to be particularly masculine or replicate their fathers' characteristics. Rather, what was influential on their development was the quality of the father–son relationship. Where this relationship was close and warm there was an influence and its outcome was an increased likelihood that boys would emulate societal norms and prevailing definitions of masculinity (Lamb, 1996). Thus, contrary to expectations, the quality of the relationship was more influential than its quantity. Children with such good relationships with their fathers were reported as well to be more psychologically well-adjusted, to do better at school, to engage in less antisocial behaviour and have more successful intimate adult relationships (Lamb, 1996).

None the less, studies of the development of pre-schoolers have also found that those with fathers providing as much as 40% of their care *"demonstrate more cognitive competence, increased empathy, fewer sex stereotypes beliefs and more internal locus of control"* (Kraemer, 1995a). Kraemer suggests that these children not only experience *"a greater richness of caretaking"* but they also see how the parent/couple relationship works, *"at times loving, at times hating or just 'getting on'"* (Kraemer, 1995a). However, while these children of participant fathers ascribe fewer sex-role stereotypes, they still remain highly conservative about sex-roles (Lewis, 1996). Indeed, Carlson (1982) concludes that even where fathers of pre-school age children have taken substantial responsibility for their care and household tasks this *"does not seem to have resulted in a group of non-masculine boys"*.

Three factors are thought to account for the beneficial effects seen in pre-schoolers who have experienced joint parenting. They are, that the parents display less sex-stereotyped roles, are themselves fulfilled, and are highly involved parents . The same effects are not found when fathers are obliged and have not chosen to be as involved in the care of their children.

Thus the influence of fathers on children's development, it is argued, is not acting independently but is part of a network of care and interrelated relationships. Both parental relationships within the family as well as relationships between family members and others outside it will influence the father's effect. The relationship between fathers and their children is part, therefore, of a broader network of relationships influential on children's development.

Similarly, the emotional relationship between fathers and their children is only one of the roles of fatherhood. Fathers may also be breadwinners, co-parents and husbands/partners to their child's mother. How these roles are fulfilled are part of the context in which children grow up. They influence the quality of the parenting children receive and thus children's development.

According to this perspective, researchers conclude that, while fathers do have an impact on children's development, its *specific* effect is probably limited, it is hard to discern and the causal mechanisms are by no means fully explained (Lewis, 1996). Moreover, if there are differences in the influences on children's development of mothers and of fathers they are not easy to measure and the effect they were once assumed to have on child development (such as boys' masculinity) has not been demonstrated (Lewis, 1996).

But this is not to say that fathers are not significant in their children's lives or are redundant to their development. Particular emphasis is placed on the quality of the parent–child relationship and such relationships may be more likely and easier to sustain when children and fathers live together. But they are not guaranteed by co-residence nor invariably absent when children and their fathers live apart.

None the less, children whose fathers are non-resident are likely to receive less of a number of the elements that foster their optimum development and the emotional relationship between fathers and their children may suffer. There may be, for example, conflict or strained relations between parents, and parenting may be reduced in quality and quantity as a result. The benefits of co-parenting and support from a partner are also lost, while financial hardship which is a frequent consequence of lone parenthood, may similarly affect non-resident fathers.

When fathers are non-resident, mothers' behaviour may itself change to affect children's development. They may, for example, take on some of the parenting role of the non-resident father, be more egalitarian in their parenting between boys and girls, and similarly ask the children to be more involved in the household chores (Biller, 1987; Mott, 1994).

Outcomes for children

The debate about non-resident fatherhood and its consequences for children is complex and controversial. Its effects differ for children of different ages and gender, as well as by their varied family experiences (see Burghes, 1994; Chase-Lansdale *et al.*, 1996; Cherlin *et al.*, 1991 and 1995; Hawkins *et al.*, 1991; McAllister, 1995; Morrison and Cherlin, 1995). Today the focus of concern is on fathers' non-residence because of parental divorce and whether as a result their children will have reduced academic and (later) occupational achievement, be more likely to engage in delinquent behaviour, enter into less-secure relationships and become parents at younger ages than children who live with both their father and mother.

Both in the United Kingdom and the United States research suggests that the average outcomes for groups of children whose parents separate are less good than are those for children whose parents stay together. By contrast, children in widowed lone-parent families often – although there are exceptions – do not fare markedly worse than their peers in intact families (Burghes, 1994; Elliott and Richards, 1991; Kiernan, 1992b; Sweeting and West, 1996).

There are several important caveats to these findings (Burghes, 1994). First, the differences between the groups of children and young people are small, even though they are statistically significant and replicated in a number of studies. Second, in many cases only a minority of the more disadvantaged group will have experienced the outcome under investigation or score badly on it (Ní Bhrolcháin *et al.*, 1994; Cherlin *et al.*, 1995). For example, Cherlin and colleagues (1995) found that few young people whose parents had divorced left home because of friction, or had a baby before marrying. Nor were most of them found to be *"hesitant to marry"*.

To put it another way, the reported average outcomes which are for groups of children and young people do not imply a straightforward relationship between children's experience of family life and their development nor an inevitable path that any child will follow because of that experience. Those who do experience some setbacks will not necessarily experience poor results on all the outcomes researched and some difficulties experienced in childhood may improve over time. While for some children poorer outcomes can be observed even before their parents' divorce, for others difficulties may not appear until their adolescence or early adulthood.

It is not possible here to explore the processes – psychological, social and financial – underlying father non-residence and children's development (Burghes, 1994). It is not known, for example, what mitigating effect a continuing good relationship between fathers and their children might have, or the benefits of co-operative and shared parenting for children post-divorce (Burghes, 1994; Simpson *et al.*, 1995; Utting, 1995). Father absence should not, however, be assumed to be invariably negative; it may indeed be positive when children have been subject to violence or abuse and children may also have alternative and positive male role models available to them (Lamb, 1981).

Concern is also expressed about father non-residence and the possibility of increased risks of delinquent and criminal behaviour among young men. Research findings do indicate an association between father non-residence as a result of parental separation and divorce and juvenile offending, although the statistical associations are often modest or weak (Junger-Tas, 1994; Utting *et al.*, 1993). Considerable weight is attached to the influence of parenting on children's behaviour – the nature and consistency of the care provided – as well as the relationship between parents and their children and the relationship between parents themselves (Utting *et al.*, 1993). The Dutch criminologist Junger-Tas has argued that *"internal family dynamics are considerably more important than family structure in affecting delinquency"* (Junger-Tas, 1994). More specifically Farrington (1994) identifies three aspects of parenting influential on their children's behaviour: discipline (which should not be excessively harsh or inconsistent), supervision (children's whereabouts and activities should be monitored) and parental attitude to their children (which should be warm and loving). Family breakdown and non-resident fatherhood make it more difficult for parents to establish and maintain the protective parenting and family relationships with their children. But in themselves they do not preclude such parenting and there are circumstances – when there is intense conflict in the family, for example – when the reverse may be the case. In the United States, for example, higher rates of juvenile offending were found in conflictual intact families than for boys with affectionate lone mothers (Farrington, 1996).

Child support

Non-resident fathers are legally bound by the Child Support Act 1991 to provide financially for their children (see also Chapter 3). The Act aims to increase the proportion of non-resident fathers paying child support for their children and increase the average amounts paid (Burghes, 1991). Its success in doing so has been limited to date. Of the Child Support Agency's 'live' cases in (November) 1996 for which a full maintenance (i.e. child support) assessment had been made, the average assessment for 'absent' (i.e. non-resident) parents who had an earned income (a half of the cases) was just over £39 a week; for all absent parents the average was just under £22 a week (Department of Social Security, 1997). Average assessments have declined over time as the assessment formula has been amended since the introduction of the 1991 Act. While not directly comparable, it is interesting to note that the average child support payment reported by lone mothers prior to the Child Support Act was £30 a week (Bradshaw and Millar, 1991).

Nor is child support invariably paid whether in full or part (Speed and Kent, 1996). The proportion of lone mothers who report receiving child support regularly has not increased over time and was around a third or less in both 1989 and 1994 (Bradshaw and Millar, 1991; Marsh et al., 1997). By comparison almost 6 in 10 of the non-resident fathers in the 1996 survey by Bradshaw et al., (1997) said that they were currently making payments and just over three-quarters that they had ever done so; most non-resident fathers also reported giving informal support (whether in money or kind).

The Child Support Agency's analysis of compliance shows that in November 1996, just over a quarter of non-resident parents for whom there had been a full maintenance (child support) assessment and payment was via the CSA collection service, were paying the full amount, one third were paying a part of this amount and the remainder were not paying anything at all (Department of Social Security, 1996). While the payment of child support by fathers does not grant them rights of contact with their children, in a recent survey a half of non-resident fathers said they would be less likely to pay the full amount of maintenance assessed if they lost contact with their children (Bradshaw et al., 1997).

Further complications and calls on the finances of fathers are added when second families are formed. This will be all the more so if their new partner already has children living with her and/or the 'new' couple subsequently have children of their own. An assumption underlying the Child Support Act 1991 is that any stepchildren will have the support of their own biological father, and that their stepfather's priority is to make financial provision for any children from a first family from whom he is now living apart. Compliance rates suggest, however, that payment cannot be assumed (see above). Non-resident fathers have clearly felt the financial needs of their second families to have been insufficiently taken into account by the Child Support Act 1991 (Maclean, 1996). Indeed, a number of changes have since been made to the child support formula to take more account of step-family responsibilities (Craig *et al.*, 1996).

Summary

Contact between fathers and their children tends to diminish when they no longer live together. This does not necessarily reflect a lack of interest by fathers in their children. Rather, it may result from psychological, social, financial and geographical constraints. Even when contact between fathers and children continues, both its quality and quantity are likely to be altered. Social policy initatives could support and facilitate continuing father–child contact post-separation.

The debate about outcomes for children with non-resident fathers is both complex and controversial. Outcomes are not uniform but vary, for example, by children's age and gender, their particular family circumstances and experience of family change. Paternal warmth and nurturing are associated with positive childhood outcomes.

Parenting does not take place in a vacuum for either fathers or mothers. These findings emphasise the importance of considering the opportunities and constraints (psychological, social, structural and economic) within which a father defines and plays out his role. And whatever his role, its effect on his children is mediated by a network of other significant and influential relationships in the child's life (Lewis, 1996; McKee and O'Brien, 1982; Russell, 1983).

Note

1. Other differences between the samples may also explain the different levels of contact reported. The NCDS sample is reporting on a younger cohort of parents who may have more recently begun living apart. According to the analysis of non-response by non-resident fathers to their survey by Bradshaw *et al.*, (1997), non-respondents were less likely to be single and unmarried and more likely to be from manual social classes than those who were interviewed.

7 Supporting fatherhood

Today, arguably, fathers and mothers are expected to share breadwinning with caring for their children and doing the domestic chores, even if attitudes vary about how parents should divide these tasks between them. In whatever way they do so, fulfilling them all can undoubtedly be difficult for parents and families may be unreasonably stressed as a result (Ferri and Smith, 1996; Utting, 1995). Parents may be expected to work long hours, leaving little time for family needs, while opting for shorter hours or becoming a sole-earner family may reduce family income unacceptably (see Figure 4.4, page 50).

Families may need more support if they are to reconcile these conflicting demands. This begs the questions of 'what support?' and 'from where?' While the type of support offered will depend on how the role of fatherhood is perceived (what it is considered appropriate for fathers to do), whether provision is public or private will reflect how governments and employers view their roles with regard to the labour market and employees and the benefits for them of supporting fatherhood. This chapter looks at a number of aspects of support for fatherhood and recent changes to these.

State financial support

Financial support for families with children has been channelled through both the taxation and social security systems. Originally the tax system reflected the breadwinning role assigned to men both as husbands – through the married man's tax allowance (subsequently the married couple's allowance) – and as fathers through entitlement to child tax allowances. Changes have been made to both allowances. By 1979 the child tax allowance had been phased out following the introduction in 1977 of child benefit (usually paid to the mother) which replaced family allowances. Moreover, apart from an increase to £1,790 in 1996-97, the married couple's allowance had remained at £1,720 since 1990-91 and now is available only at the 15% rate of taxation (Saunders and Smailes, 1996). This has been justified in part because wives are now taxed independently from their husbands, and as women are increasingly likely to be in employment there is no longer the same presumption that a wife is entirely financially dependent on her husband. It has been argued that the revenue 'savings' accrued from freezing the married couple's tax allowance should be used to provide increased support for children, but this has not taken place and the real value of child benefit has also been eroded over time (Child Poverty Action Group, 1995b).

The overall effect of changes in taxation, National Insurance and child benefit for families can be seen in Table 7.1. The figures show a shift to the disadvantage of families with children, and this is particularly true of those who are lower paid. The proportion of income paid in tax and National Insurance contributions more than doubled, for example, for low- and middle-income families with children – those with between a half and average male earnings – between 1964-65 and 1994-45 and have improved only fractionally since. Indeed, the increase (in the tax/NI take) has been fourfold for those with the lowest incomes. Even those with between twice and five times average earnings experienced proportionate increases of between a third up to almost a half. It is only at earnings 10 times the average that there has been a marked fall in income tax and National Insurance as a proportion of gross earnings. The figures also show that lower-income families with children are no longer in as advantageous a position compared with those without children as once was the case.

Table 7.1   Tax and National Insurance contributions as a proportion of gross earnings

Proportion of average male earnings	Half	Three-quarters	Average	Twice	Five times	Ten times
single person	%	%	%	%	%	%
1964-65	14.7	19.8	23.1	26.6	29.8	42.3
1978-79	23.6	28.9	31.5	33.7	52.2	67.5
1994-95	22.2	26.4	28.6	32.1	36.8	38.4
1995-96	22.1	26.4	28.5	32.0	36.8	38.4
1996-97	21.3	25.5	27.6	31.2	36.5	38.2
married no children						
1964-65	8.5	14.3	18.6	24.4	28.2	41.2
1978-79	16.0	23.8	27.8	31.4	50.5	66.5
1994-95	18.6	24.1	26.8	31.2	36.5	38.3
1995-96	19.5	24.7	27.2	31.4	36.6	38.3
1996-97	18.7	23.8	26.3	30.6	36.2	38.1
married couple 2 children (under 11) one earner						
1964-65	2.2	4.0	9.0	19.3	26.8	39.5
1978-79	2.5	14.6	20.9	27.9	48.8	65.5
1994-95	8.8	17.5	21.9	28.7	35.5	37.7
1995-96	9.6	18.1	22.3	28.9	35.6	37.8
1996-97	8.8	17.2	21.4	28.1	35.2	37.6

Note: Child benefit included.

Source: Utting, D. (1995) and House of Commons Hansard, 28 February 1996, cols 366-70

These changes may reflect shifts in attitudes about both fathers' roles and that of the state. Financial support for fatherhood was greater when expectations of fatherhood focused on their role as family breadwinner. Now it may be thought more appropriate to help parents meet the cost of raising their children rather than specifically supporting the father in providing for his children, although the decline in financial support for fatherhood may have been the indirect consequence of some other policy development, such as the move to independent taxation or reducing the burden of taxation on the higher-paid.

It has been argued that changes to fiscal policy have produced a situation in which married-couple families are treated less favourably than lone-parent families, and that lone-parent families are at a financial advantage as a result (Morgan, 1995). This is a controversial and complex debate which it is not possible to explore here. Both the argument that lone parents are 'better off', however and, if they are, the consequences of their financial advantage for family formation have been challenged (Berthoud and Ford, 1996; Dickens, Fry and Pashardes, 1995; Pappenheim, 1997).

None the less, the argument that changes in fiscal support have influenced family formation and encouraged lone parenthood over the two-parent family has had an impact on public policy (Roberts (1996). As a result, and in order to *"equalise the treatment of one- and two-parent families"*, reductions in lone parents' entitlement to benefit were announced by the Conservative Government in the November 1996 Budget (Pappenheim, 1997). While existing claimants were to have their entitlement to one-parent benefit and the Income Support lone parent premium frozen, benefit entitlement was to be abolished for new claimants. These changes were due to come into effect in April 1998; their fate is uncertain as a result of the election of the Labour Government on 1 May 1997.

A further effect of the interaction of taxes and National Insurance with means-tested benefits is the creation of *poverty* and *unemployment traps* (see Boxes below and over), which make it difficult for low-paid and unemployed fathers to improve their family finances through employment.

The poverty trap and plateau

The poverty trap and the poverty plateau refer to those circumstances where increases in gross earnings bring little or no gain in net earnings. In each case, gains in (gross) earnings are all but, or entirely, offset by extra tax, National Insurance payments and reductions in entitlement to means-tested benefits. For example, in 1995 a married couple with two young children and one full-time employee gained no more than £10 a week in their net income after housing costs for any increase in their weekly gross earnings between £120 and £235 a week (Department of Social Security, 1995d, Table 1.7).

Some families are more at risk than others of one or either of these 'traps'. Those without educational or occupational qualifications or work experience, for example, are particularly likely to be caught by the unemployment trap because they are more likely to be restricted to low pay. Similarly, because they are more likely than other families to be entitled to means-tested benefits, families with children are most risk of being caught in the poverty trap (Parker, 1995). On the other hand, families may be unaware of either the poverty or unemployment trap or, if they are, may not allow them to influence their behaviour.

The unemployment trap

At low pay levels, income net of tax, National Insurance and other work-related costs may be little more than that available from out-of-work social security benefits, even when in-work social security benefits have been taken into account.

In practice, the unemployment trap operates only at very low earnings levels for fathers with children. For a family living in local authority housing with two children under 11 years old, for example, gross earnings as low as £36 a week provide an income equivalent to their income support entitlement when out of work, providing they claim all the in-work benefit to which they are entitled (Department of Social Security, 1995d, Table 3.2).

While the earnings needed to match the income support level for unemployed fathers and their families rises with family size, the weekly amounts are still modest. The in-work income of a couple with four children (aged 3, 8, 11 and 16), for example, will match their unemployment income support entitlement at weekly earnings of around £70 a week.

Work costs (travel, clothing, equipment) are not taken into account in these calculations and increase the gross earnings needed to match out-of-work social security entitlement. Similarly, owner-occupiers (two-thirds of small families and more than a half of large families) face a greater financial hurdle in moving from out-of-work to in-work incomes (Office of Population Censuses and Surveys, 1996).[1]

In addition, fathers who are owner-occupiers and low paid and whose wives are in employment are less likely be able to benefit from the recently introduced child-care allowance (now up to £60 a week) to help overcome the unemployment trap because those receiving maximum family credit do not have housing benefit entitlement against which it can be offset.

Employment rights and conditions

This section looks at a number of aspects of employment rights and conditions of employment and fatherhood – these include *paternity* and *parental leave schemes*, *leave for family reasons*, *family-friendly* and *flexible employment* conditions and *hours of work*. The section is divided in three, looking first at public policy – where comparisons with developments in Europe are also drawn and the costs of statutory schemes reviewed – then at employer provision, and finally the demand for and use of employment leave schemes is considered.

Public policy and provision

Public policy for fathers arguably reflects the importance the state attaches to the involvement of fathers in their children's upbringing and its own role in making possible that involvement (Employment Committee, 1995a; O'Brien, 1995).

The development of parental and paternity leave schemes also reflects a recognition of the changing roles of fathers and mothers and the consequences of these changes (Bell *et al.*, 1983; Conference of European Ministers, 1995; Exploring Parenthood, 1995;

O'Brien, 1995). Indeed, parental leave schemes that are 'father-sensitive' are more likely in countries with a tradition of full-time employment among mothers (O'Brien, 1995).

Neither the case for, nor the provision of, statutory parental and paternity leave have yet made much headway in Britain. In this regard Britain stands as the odd one out among her European partners (see below) and little lead has been shown or support given for more involvement by fathers in the care of their children (O'Brien, 1995). Indeed, the Conservative Government opposed to the introduction of any statutory entitlement to either unpaid parental leave or family leave (Employment Committee 1995b). Their arguments against included the costs these would impose on employers, a concern to reduce employment legislation, the increasing availability of voluntarily developed schemes (see below) (Daniels, 1995; Employment Committee, 1995b) and a belief that these policies should be negotiated at the workplace between employers and employees (see below).

A more positive approach, to parental leave at least, is expected from the current Labour government. Some commentators argue that, as far as direct employer-employee negotiations are concerned, collective bargaining has historically played a greater role in Britain than in Europe in the negotiation of employee entitlements. Whether or not this is the case, in the absence of statutory provision, its relative importance has been greater and the trade union movement has certainly been active in developing and negotiating policies even if these have not been highly visible in the public arena (Trades Union Congress, 1996b).

This apparent lack of support for pro-father policies is in contrast to earlier policy developments around the employment of mothers, which witnessed a much more supportive pro-legislative climate in the 1970s, the enactment of specific pro-work maternity rights and equal opportunities legislation and a popular movement in support of these developments. None the less there is also evidence of some growing support for the involvement of fathers in their children's lives (APPGP, 1994; Employment Committee, 1995a). Alan Howarth MP, a member of the All-Party Parliamentary Group on Parenting, suggested, for example, that *"paternity leave will prove to be a very good investment indeed on the part of society"* (*Guardian*, 1994).

i) Paternity leave

Unlike parental leave, which enables either parent to take time off work to care for their children, paternity leave entitles fathers to take time off work, usually around the time of the child's birth (Moss, 1994). Paternity leave schemes in Europe are more of a rarity than are parental leave schemes (Figure 7.1) – only seven countries out of the 15 have paternity leave schemes. These seven also have parental leave schemes. Paternity leave is less likely than parental leave to be paid; in just four countries – Austria, Denmark, Finland and Sweden – both parental and paternity leave are paid at least in part, while leave is unpaid in Belgium, France and Spain (European Commission Network on Childcare, 1996).

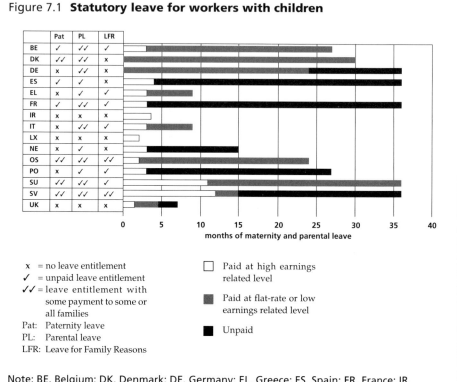

Figure 7.1 **Statutory leave for workers with children**

	Pat	PL	LFR
BE	✓	✓✓	✓
DK	✓✓	✓✓	x
DE	x	✓✓	x
ES	✓	✓	x
EL	x	✓	✓
FR	✓	✓✓	✓
IR	x	x	x
IT	x	✓✓	✓
LX	x	x	x
NE	x	✓	x
OS	✓✓	✓✓	✓✓
PO	x	✓	✓
SU	✓✓	✓✓	✓
SV	✓✓	✓✓	✓✓
UK	x	x	x

months of maternity and parental leave

x = no leave entitlement
✓ = unpaid leave entitlement
✓✓ = leave entitlement with
      some payment to some or
      all families
Pat: Paternity leave
PL: Parental leave
LFR: Leave for Family Reasons

☐ Paid at high earnings
    related level

▨ Paid at flat-rate or low
    earnings related level

■ Unpaid

Note: BE, Belgium; DK, Denmark; DE, Germany; EL, Greece; ES, Spain; FR, France; IR, Ireland; IT, Italy; LX, Luxembourg; NE, Netherlands; OS, Austria; PO, Portugal; SU, Finland, SV, Sweden; UK, United Kingdom.

Source: European Commission Network on Childcare (1996).

A Review of Services for Young Children in the European Union 1990-1995.

ii) Parental leave

The European Commission Directive on Parental Leave, first submitted in 1983, when phased in (see Box below), will guarantee employed mothers and fathers at least three months' (unpaid) leave (Moss, 1994). However, as Britain originally opted out of its adoption, the Directive on Parental Leave does not yet apply in the United Kingdom. The Labour government is expected to reverse this decision and implement the policy over a transitional period, possibly of up to two years.

Elsewhere in Europe it is now the norm for countries to have statutory parental leave schemes (Figure 7.1) and only three countries – Ireland, Luxembourg and the United Kingdom – out of 15 do not. Moreover, in 8 of the 12 countries at least a proportion of the leave is paid for, either at a flat-rate or earnings-related – whether at a high or low level. There is considerable variation in other aspects of these parental leave schemes such as their duration and when, how and by whom the leave may be taken (European Commission Network on Childcare, 1996).

> **The Directive on Parental Leave and the Council of Ministers' Recommendation on Childcare**
>
> The Directive on Parental Leave adopted by the Council of Ministers in March 1996 lays down minimum parental leave standards. It "entitles ... men and women workers to an individual right to parental leave on the grounds of the birth or adoption of a child to enable them to take care of the child, for at least three months ... To promote equal opportunities and equal treatment between men and women ... parental leave ... should, in principle, be granted on a non-transferable basis" (quoted in Moss, 1996). Member states have two years (or three in special circumstances) to implement the Directive (Trades Union Congress, 1996b).
>
> In addition the Council of Ministers Recommendation on Childcare was adopted by all member states in 1992. It is not, however, legally binding. One objective of the Recommendation is to encourage government initiatives which will support the increased participation by men in the care of their children (Moss, 1996).

iii) Leave for family reasons

A number of European countries also offer leave for family reasons (Figure 7.1), which allows parents to take time off to care for their sick children. The leave may be paid or supported by entitlement to means-tested benefits but is more commonly unpaid (Conference of European Ministers, 1995; European Commission Network on Childcare, 1996). Only eight European countries (Austria, Belgium, Finland, France, Greece, Italy, Portugal and Sweden) currently have schemes offering leave for family reasons. Family leave schemes tend to go hand-in-hand with parental and paternity leave schemes; five of the eight countries with family leave schemes also have parental and paternal leave policies.

iv) Working hours

A European Union Directive on the organisation of working time adopted by the Council of Ministers in 1993 lays down minimum requirements for workers'[2] rest entitlement and maximum working periods (see Box below) – notably a maximum working week, including overtime, of 48 hours (averaged over four months). Voluntary agreements may be made with employers by employees who voluntarily wish to work more than 48 hours a week. The Directive was unsuccessfully opposed by the former Conservative government, it will be implemented by the current Labour administration.

In the United Kingdom working long weekly hours is more common than in other European countries (see Chapter 4). Other Member States are also more likely to already have statutory controls concerning working time. According to the European Commission, the statutory working week is 48 hours in Germany, Ireland, Italy, The Netherlands and Portugal, 40 hours in Belgium, Spain and Luxembourg and 39 hours in France (European Commission, 1996).

European Directive on the Organisation of Working Time

The right to daily rest

- a minimum daily rest period of 11 consecutive hours per 24-hour period

- a rest break if the working day is longer than six hours

- night work not exceeding an average eight hours in any 24-hour period

The right to weekly rest

- a minimum 35-hour uninterrupted rest period per each 7-day period (averaged over two weeks)

- a maximum working week, including overtime of 48 hours averaged over four months

The right to weekly rest

- a minimum four weeks paid annual leave a year.

Source: European Commission, 1996.

Cost of statutory schemes

Estimates of the cost of proposed parental, paternity or family leave schemes vary depending on assumptions about provision – whether leave will be paid or unpaid, and for how long, for example – and the extent of their take-up by those entitled to them (Holtermann, 1995). Holtermann (1995) estimates, for example, the cost (in 1992-93) of paying the equivalent of the basic rate statutory maternity pay to employees with at least six months of National Insurance contributions for 13 weeks of parental leave to all parents, five days of leave for family reasons and five days of paternity leave. The respective costs for these leave entitlements were between £130 million and £170 million (depending on take-up), £35 million and £25 million.

A study of parental leave policies in 17 developed countries between 1966 and 1988 calculated that while lengthy leave periods reduced employment, periods of leave that were short to moderate (paid and unpaid) actually increased both employment and incomes (Ruhm and Teague, 1995 cited in Balls, 1996; Wilkinson and Briscoe, 1996).

Estimates of the costs of leave schemes need, as well, to take account of less-visible savings. In the case of employers, for example, parents without any designated leave entitlement may take unsanctioned personal sick leave to care for children who fall ill. Similarly, there may be less-tangible costs from insufficient or inadequate parenting when parents are unable to take necessary leave to look after their children (Wilkinson and Briscoe, 1996).

In their presentation of cost estimates of the implementation of the Working Time Directive in the UK, the Department of Trade and Industry (DTI) warns that *"cost estimates can be no more than indicative and, to some extent speculative"*. The DTI analysis of the cost of the Directive suggests that rest periods and possible increases in minimum leave account for the greater part of the cost with that of the 48-hour working provision, itself estimated at £100 million a year (Department of Trade and Industry, 1996).

Employer provision

i) Paternity and parental leave

While Britain has neither statutory paternity nor parental leave schemes, some employers do offer such schemes to their employees. Evidence of the availability of such schemes is piecemeal and contradictory, probably reflecting differences in survey coverage. The 1994 British Social Attitudes Survey found paternity leave available to a third of men with a child under 12 years (Thomson, 1995). Similarly, Holtermann and Clarke (1992) found that about a quarter of employers surveyed had paternity leave schemes, although the length of leave was often very short and schemes were very varied in other respects. However, a 1994 survey by Industrial Relations Services reported 70% of the 365 companies surveyed to have a paternity leave scheme but this was not a random sample of all employers (Industrial Relations Services, 1994).

Common, none the less, to the findings from both Holtermann and Clark (1992) and Industrial Relations Services (1994) is the variation in what the schemes offered. While some schemes were a contractual right of employees, others offered leave only at the employer's discretion. Leave might be paid or unpaid, was of variable duration and might have to be taken at a specific time or within a given period of time.

The surveys thus highlight one of the drawbacks of negotiated voluntary agreements, namely that not all fathers are guaranteed access to leave schemes or minimum leave conditions. Moreover, such voluntary developments are thought to be more likely in the public sector and among larger established companies with entitlement still discretionary. Employees in small firms may not fare so well (Employment Committee, 1995a).

Despite the British government's opt-out from the European Directive on Parental Leave, the Confederation of British Industry believes that many of its member companies with European interests will accept the leave provisions (*Financial Times*, 1995). This is, in some respects, provision through the back door as British companies with operations in Europe extend to their British workforce the parental leave that their European counterparts are entitled to take under the Parental Leave Directive. Similarly, it is thought that other European employers (as a result of the Framework Agreement on Parental Leave drawn up between those European employers and trade unions) will extend to their UK employees parental leave entitlement available to their own (European) workforce (Burgess and Ruxton, 1996). Paternity leave entitlement is also sometimes becoming available to fathers as developments in employers' equal opportunities programmes give employed fathers equal rights with employed mothers and Brannen *et al.*, (1995) cite two surveys reporting availability and/or use of family-friendly practices by the men to be *"more common in organisations with higher proportions of women workers"*. However, when paternal leave schemes are introduced in this way, employers may be less committed to them as a 'real benefit' (Burgess and Ruxton, 1996; New Ways to Work, 1995).

ii) Family-friendly and flexible employment

In addition to the leave policies discussed above, family-friendly and flexible employ-ment policies may enable fathers to spend more time caring for their children even if they are not designed specifically to this end. They include, for example, career breaks and the opportunity both to work less than full-time as well as to work flexibly and job-share (Daniels, 1995).

Data from the 1994 British Social Attitudes Survey reveals that of a range of flexible working practices flexible hours and working from home were most likely to be avail-able to and be taken up by fathers; almost 4 in 10 fathers were able to work flexible hours and almost a third did so. Similarly, almost a quarter of fathers were able to work at home and almost 1 in 5 did so (Thomson, 1995).

Family-friendly and flexible policies tend, however, to be confined to large em-ployers and are more likely to be available to mothers than to fathers. They make economic sense for the employer who otherwise may lose his trained female staff on motherhood (Cooper and Lewis, 1995; Daniels, 1995; Employment Committee, 1995a). But it does not help fathers to share more in the care of their children nor dual-earner families to spread between them the stress of juggling work and family demands. It is mothers, moreover, who as a result *"get labelled as being 'that difficult bunch' who have to have special benefits"*, while parenting is not seen as a responsibility shared by mothers and fathers (Daniels, 1995).

The overall impression is that government- and employer-initiated policies are overwhelmingly focused on mothers rather than fathers and that *"'Family friendly' often means in practice helping women to carry an unequal share of family responsibilities, rather than promoting more equal sharing of responsibilities between men and women"* (Hogg and Harker, 1992).

As with parental leave, fathers are more reluctant than are mothers to make use of these schemes, because the career culture, with its emphasis on continuous attendance at work, militates against them doing so (Cooper and Lewis, 1995).

Demand for and use of employment leave

While their cost is one argument against paternity and parental leave schemes, another advanced is that few fathers make use of them when they are available. But much de-pends on the nature of the scheme and take-up may be low because leave is unpaid or low paid (Bell *et al.*, 1993; Carlsen, 1995; Moss, 1994). Take-up of leave may improve over time as it becomes more acceptable to do so – this has been the experience in Sweden – and it probably cannot improve unless there is both an entitlement to take it which therefore protects fathers, income to go with it and a social and employment culture in which it is acceptable for fathers to take paternity leave.

In the first year that a parental leave scheme gave Swedish fathers the opportunity to stay home and look after their children – some 20 years ago – only 2% did so; the proportion is now 40% although they take only 15% of the parental insurance benefit days available to them (Wilkinson and Briscoe, 1996). One month of the parental leave period is now reserved for fathers to encourage further take-up (Conference of European Ministers, 1995). Moreover, nearly all fathers in Sweden take paternity leave (Hogg and Harker, 1992).

Fathers' use of parental leave may itself depend on whether parental leave is transferable between mothers and fathers as well as on the length of maternity leave. In Sweden, for example, apart from the one month of parental leave set aside for fathers, much parental leave is thought to be taken by mothers, frequently as a way of extending their maternity leave to continue breast-feeding (Lewis, 1986). In other words, *"very few men take full opportunity of the leave that is available to them"* (Lewis, 1995b) even if they make more use of it than do their peers in other countries. In Bavaria (Germany) and Denmark, for example, fathers are similarly reported to make only limited use of transferable parental leave (Trades Union Congress, 1996b; Wilkinson and Briscoe, 1996).

Even when fathers are entitled to take leave, they may find it difficult to do so because of the pressure of work, the negative attitude of their employer or the fear that doing so will jeopardise their employment prospects (Bell, 1983; Collins and Walton; 1995; Conference of European Ministers, 1995; Cooper and Lewis, 1995; Moss, 1994; United Nations, 1994). These may be among the reasons why fathers are more likely to take paternity leave than parental leave (Carlsen, 1995; O'Brien, 1995).

Evidence from the 1994 British Social Attitudes Survey suggests that fathers of young children (under 12 years) do make use of paternity leave when it is available to them; thus paternity leave was available to 36% of those interviewed and 29% of fathers had made use of it. An even larger proportion of fathers were able to take time to care for sick children – 49% – and 33% had done so. Of fathers who did not have these leave entitlements, 50% said that they would make use of paternity scheme and 40% would take time off to care for sick children were they able to do so (Thomson, 1995).

Even in the absence of statutory paternity or parental leave and variable employer provision, fathers in Britain do take time off when their children are born; they may do so unofficially, using holiday entitlement or by taking sick leave (Bell et al., 1983). A survey of just under 300 fathers found that more than a quarter took some time off, not only at the birth of their child but during the pregnancy and in the post-natal period as well. They had often to use their annual leave to do so, even when their employer was sympathetic. A fifth of these fathers lost pay as a result of the time taken off and the amounts were sometimes substantial (Bell et al., 1983).

Summary

Fatherhood is frequently acclaimed, both popularly and politically and its importance discussed. But this praise is not always matched with tangible support, through either fiscal, employment or social policy. Indeed, such support is often conspicuous by its absence as is the case with the lack of any such government commitment to statutory parental leave.

Changes in taxation and social security have reduced the financial support received by men both as husbands and as fathers. As a result, less financial support is received by families with children than was once the case and fathers with lower earnings have been affected particularly badly.

Fathers who are out of work may be caught in the unemployment trap, which makes it difficult for them to earn a sufficient income to match their out-of-work benefit entitlement once all the costs of going to work are taken into account. This is a greater problem for fathers who are owner-occupiers and for those with larger families. Fathers may also find that their ability to increase their incomes is restricted by the poverty trap; income increases are limited or nil when earnings rise, because of the simultaneous reductions in their social security benefits and the increase in their taxation and National Insurance liability.

Even if the provision of parental and paternity leave schemes by employers is increasing, in the absence of a statutory requirement to provide paternity and parental leave entitlement to such leave will not be guaranteed to all fathers since it will be at their employers' discretion to do so.

Nor, however, is the provision of entitlement to leave a guarantee that fathers will take it. Personal, cultural, economic and institutional factors may militate against them doing so. None the less, those fathers who would like to spend more time with and looking after their children will be able to do so only if they have actual access to paternal or parental leave provisions, whether these are publicly or privately provided, and do not incur social opprobrium if they take it.

Notes

1. Owner-occupiers with mortgages can have the full amount of their interest payments met when they have been unemployed for 16 weeks and are receiving income support. However, no financial help is available for low-paid employed owner-occupiers working 16 hours or more a week, and once in work they will again be expected to make both interest and capital repayments (as well as accrued capital debt repayments).

2. Some workers are not covered by the provisions of the Directive. See European Commission (1996).

8 Conclusions and policy implications

This has been a broad-brush look at fathers and fatherhood in Britain today and it has not been possible to do justice to every aspect of it. Moreover, informed discussion about fathers and fatherhood is hampered by an absence of regularly published official statistics. Unlike women, men who have children are not routinely distinguished in official statistics from those who do not. Within these limitations, what does this review tell us about fathers and fatherhood in Britain today? In any summary of the findings, the visibility, diversity and contradictions of current fatherhood feature as well as the structural changes taking place in fathers' lives.

The visibility of fatherhood

Visibility reflects both the proliferation of interest and the extent to which this is increasingly made public through the media, where fathers are often portrayed as either heroes or villains. Regrettably also there are only limited accounts of fatherhood from fathers themselves so we know little about what fathering means to them, or how they feel about the changing expectations of fatherhood or the structural changes in which it takes place.

Diversity of fatherhood

Family change

Diversity encompasses both demographic change and competing models of fatherhood. Family change – both the increase in fathers living apart from their children as well as the breakdown in and diversity of parenting partnerships – has understandably dominated much of the recent debate around fatherhood. Between 1 in 6 and 1 in 7 fathers live apart from some or all of their dependent children and fathers may, for example, be married, never-married, no longer married or re-married. In addition, they may be biological or social fathers whether in intact, lone or reconstituted families (Chapter 2).

This public concentration on change and diversity in fatherhood has tended, however, to obscure its continuity. Almost all fathers are married and most (85%) continue to live with all of their dependent biological children (Chapter 2).

Competing models of fatherhood

The increasing diversity of fatherhood has come at a time when the debate about the nature of fatherhood is also in full swing. What fathers do or do not do is frequently debated, as well as what it is thought they should do. It has often been assumed that fatherhood is confined to breadwinning and that a caring role is eschewed. The reality both is and was historically more complex; no doubt breadwinning fathers did and do nurture, and nurturing fathers are and will be breadwinners.

A key emphasis today is on increasing the nurturing role of fatherhood. There are calls, for example, whether in the media, by politicians or academics, for fathers to be more involved in their children's lives, to have close, caring and emotionally involved relationships with them (Kraemer, 1995b and 1995c). But while in the past the defining role of fatherhood as breadwinning seemed straightforward, quite what comprises the 'new' fatherhood is less certain. As Moss (1995) suggests, *"what fatherhood was is perhaps fairly clear, what it might become is less so."*

Nor is fathers' breadwinning role negligible. Fathers in general remain the major breadwinners alongside an increasing economic contribution by mothers to family income. The reality, therefore, may be a shift in the complementary roles of fathers and mothers: an increase in the nurturing role of fathers and the breadwinning role of mothers. Neither should be overemphasised. Both fathers and mothers now do more of the role traditionally assigned to the other without either having acceded the more traditional role divisions.

Contradictions in fatherhood

Contradictions are evident both in the growing divide between models of the 'new' fatherhood and family change as well as in the legal representations of fatherhood.

The call for father–child relationships to be 'closer' and more nurturing has come just as fatherhood has become more diverse, and more fathers and their children are living apart from one another. This is the first contradiction. For non-resident fathers, close, involved fathering presents an even greater challenge than it does for fathers in intact families who, even so, may face structural, cultural, institutional and economic barriers to forming such relationships with their children. On the other hand, fathers may unjustifiably claim these barriers impede their greater involvement with their children when they are no more than an excuse for their failure to do so (Chapter 5).

Much attention focuses on non-resident and absent fatherhood and its repercussions on child outcomes, juvenile behaviour and adult family formation (Chapter 6). If fathers who do not live with their children are to provide the perceived benefits of close fathering, the particular additional practical difficulties such fathers face will need to be addressed. Men may also face the challenging task of being social fathers to stepchildren. Here norms about their fathering role are even less clearly defined than is the case for biological fatherhood.

The second contradiction is the representation of fatherhood in law. On the one hand the rights and responsibilities of fatherhood centre unequivocally around children's well-being, in for example, the Children Act 1989. By contrast it is parental financial responsibility that underlies the Child Support Act 1991 and is also combined with parental responsibility for children's behaviour in the Criminal Justice Act 1991. While the Child Support Act imposes financial responsibilities irrespective of marital status, parental responsibility is not automatically attained by unmarried fathers.

Structural changes

Structural changes are shaping the lives of both fathers and mothers. For growing numbers of parents, employment is more insecure and the labour market frequently imposes long and unsocial hours of work (Chapter 4). Family needs often require both parents to be in paid work and juggle demanding work and home responsibilities; stress is likely to increase and life satisfaction deteriorate as a result (Chapter 5).

Alongside these changes, fathers are spending more time looking after their children and (to a smaller degree) on domestic chores, and families still do spend time in activities together (Ferri and Smith, 1996). But, in general, women still spend more time on child care, and are largely responsible for the core domestic chores even when they work full-time, and retain responsibility for seeing they are done as well, while the contribution made by fathers declines as their hours of work increase.

The future of fatherhood

How fatherhood will be constructed in the future will depend on how fathers perceive their role, and the structural supports or barriers to putting this into practice. It has been argued that both men and women want more balanced lives with more time for family life and their work a less prominent influence on their lives (Cooper and Lewis, 1995; Wilkinson and Mulgan, 1995). Dench argues, however, that more traditional attitudes about the division of family responsibilities reassert themselves with the arrival of caring responsibilities (Dench, 1996a and 1996b). These differing attitudes may reflect the practical difficulty of putting more egalitarian ideals – of equal breadwinning and caring for a home and family – into practice.

Young people's views also appear to reflect the complexity of combining old and new views of fathering. O'Brien and Jones (1996) found a group of predominantly working-class young people (aged 14 years old) to

> *appear to endorse a modern 'new father' model whilst not rejecting the importance of breadwinning. ... A majority of children felt that earning money was the most important activity for fathers, followed by giving care and love and being involved in domestic duties. Seventy per cent agreed with the statement 'Children need a father to be as closely involved in their upbringing as their mother'.*

Whether these views will hold good or be changed by the experience of parent-hood and whether they will be able to put them into practice remains to be seen.

Policy implications

In the light of this review of fathers and fatherhood in Britain, what might the mini-mum parameters of a coherent policy on fathering be? A starting-point might be the acknowledgement that such a policy has been conspicuous by its absence and that key questions need to be addressed if such a policy is to be developed. They include what fatherhood is to comprise, what policies are required to support such fatherhood (and what current barriers fathers face) and who are the key players in the provision of these policies.

An essential starting-point is how fathers perceive the future of fatherhood and how this relates to the needs of mothers and children. Fatherhood comprises both di-rect and indirect roles in relation to their children – as carers and nurturers, as breadwinners and as co-parents and partners to their children's mother – with varying degrees of importance and emphasis placed on these roles by fathers. The value society places on these different elements of fatherhood will also be critical to developments in policy.

As far as the development of policy is concerned, much will depend on how both the public and private sectors view their responsibilities towards fathers and families and the advantages to them of doing so. Society in general, could, for example, be said to be a beneficiary of policies that increase children's welfare, while employers too may benefit from policies which ease the stress on their employees (both fathers and moth-ers) resulting from the conflicting and excessive demands of work and family life. What is the role for public policy? As far as employment rights and conditions are concerned, lack of intervention is sometimes justified on the grounds that such matters are for private negotiation between employers and their employees. But there are also exam-ples of public policy – notably the Child Support Act 1991 – in which the government has been active in defining the role of fathers.

As far as policy development for fathers is concerned, the key players, none the less, will be central government and employers, the European Union and the trade unions; the key issue areas include the labour market and fiscal, social and legal poli-cies. Labour market opportunities determine the availability of jobs which allow fathers to act as breadwinners and provide financial support for their families, while fiscal policy sets the level of financial support through taxation and social security. Histori-cally, society has perceived fathers' primary role as that of family breadwinner. While breadwinning may still be seen as a central role of fatherhood, arguably it is a role no longer as well supported as it was by social and fiscal policies.

None the less, it is with regard to fathers' financial provision for their children that one of the few explicit developments in policy has taken place in the past decade, with the introduction of the Child Support Act 1991. The furore created by its introduction, moreover, shows how difficult such intervention is, particularly in achieving an acceptable balance as far as fathers' financial responsibilities to first and second families are concerned. Moreover, no matter how firmly social policy holds to the view that financial support and father–child contact are not connected, recent research suggests that many non-resident fathers clearly do see such a connection (Bradshaw *et al.*, 1997).

Conditions of employment as well as fathers' employment-based rights, including hours of work, paternal, parental and/or family leave, affect how fathers are able to reconcile their work and family responsibilities and how active they are able to be in their children's daily lives. In none of these areas did the Conservative government see itself as a key player. It remains to be seen how the new Labour government put their apparently more positive approach into practice.

Policy may also need to address the particular obstacles that non-resident fathers face in their relationships with their children. Not infrequently a limited income may hamper contact with their children, as may accommodation unsuitable for children's visits, geographical distance and children's own emotional well-being. Policy initiatives might both encourage contact by assisting it and in so doing prevent non-residence becoming absence.

Arguably policy needs to promote secure attachments for all children (Kraemer, 1995d). As far as fathers and their families are concerned, policies are needed that support residential fathering, hand-in-hand with those that support continuing contact and involvement of fathers in the lives of their children (where it is appropriate to do so) when they no longer live together.

As far as fatherhood and the law is concerned, unmarried fathers remain in a number of respects disadvantaged by comparison with their married peers. Marriage bestows parental rights automatically while unmarried fathers must apply for them. Similarly, the provisions of the Family Law Act 1996 apply only to married parents, and unmarried fathers who separate and live apart from their children will not benefit from any gains made as a result of the mediation and counselling initiatives contained within it. Social policy needs to reflect, therefore, on the way in which marital status acts as a discriminating factor between fathers, whether their roles as fathers and the well-being of their children are affected for the worse as a result, and if so if this should be addressed.

The objective of policy must be to develop a coherent strategy both on and between each parameter such that fathers can fulfil and balance both breadwinning and caring roles. To do so will require a clear public statement that fathers matter. Central government also needs to pay attention to the wider impact of policies developed to meet particular issues. It is by no means novel to bemoan the lack of coherence in the development of family policy or to suggest the need for an integrated approach to developments in social policy, but that makes such coherent policy development no less essential as a result.

Bibliography

Allard, A. (1996). *Youth employment: a contradiction in terms.* London: The Children's Society.

APPGP (All-Party Parliamentary Group on Parenting and International Year of the Family UK) (1994). *Report of Parliamentary Hearings,* All-Party Parliamentary Group on Parenting and International Year of the Family UK.

Balls, E. (1996). New man faces up to parental leave dilemma. *Guardian,* 19 February.

Bayley, J., Condy, A. and Roberts, C. (eds.) (1995). *Policies for families: work, poverty and resources.* Proceedings of seminars held in 1994. London: Family Policy Studies Centre.

Bell, C., McKee, L. and Priestly, K. (1983). *Fathers, childbirth and work.* Manchester: Equal Opportunities Commission.

Berthoud, R and Ford, R. (1996). *A new way of measuring relative financial needs,* Findings, Social Policy Research 109, York: Joseph Rowntree Foundation.

Biller, H.B. (1987). The father and sex-role development. In Lamb, M.E., *The father's role in cross-cultural perspectives.* John Wiley and Sons Inc.

Booth, A. and Dunn, J. (eds.) (1994). *Stepfamilies: Who benefits? Who does not?* Lawrence Erlbaum Associates.

Bradshaw, J. (1996). Address to All-Party Committee on the Child Support Act. Social Policy Research Unit, University of York.

Bradshaw, J. and Millar, J. (1991). *Lone parent families in the UK.* Research Report No 6. Department of Social Security. HMSO.

Bradshaw, J., Stimson, C., Williams, J. and Skinner, C. (1997). Non resident fathers in Britain. Paper presented to ESRC Programme on Population and Household Change seminar, 13 March.

Brannen, J., Meszaros, G., Moss, P. and Poland, G. (1995). *Employment and family life: A review of research in the UK (1980-1994).* Research Series No. 41. Employment Department.

Buck, N., Gershuny, J., Rose, D. and Scott, J. (1994). *Changing households: the British Household Panel Survey 1990-1992.* ESRC Centre on Micro-Social Change, University of Essex.

Burgess, A. (1997). *Fatherhood reclaimed. The making of the modern father.* London: Vermillion

Burgess, A. and Ruxton, S. (1996). *Men and their children: proposals for public policy.* London: Institute for Public Policy Research.

Burghes, L. (1991). *Supporting our children: The family impact of child maintenance.* London: Family Policy Studies Centre.

Burghes, L. (1993). *One-parent families: Policy options for the 1990s.* York: Joseph Rowntree Foundation.

Burghes, L. (1994). *Lone parenthood and family disruption: The outcomes for children.* London: Family Policy Studies Centre.

Burghes, L. (1995a). Caught in the Act. *Family Policy Bulletin.* London: Family Policy Studies Centre.

Burghes, L. (1995b). *Single lone mothers: problems, prospects and policies.* Family and Parenthood series. London: Family Policy Studies Centre.

Burgoyne, J. and Clark, D. (1982). From father to stepfather. In McKee, L. and O'Brien, M. (eds.), *The father figure.* London: Tavistock Publications.

Cappuccini, G. and Cochrane, R. (1996). *Role division and gender role attitudes: couples adjusting to the arrival of their first baby*. Paper presented to British Psychological Society. September.

Carlsen, S. (1995). When working men become fathers. In Moss, P. (ed.), *Father figures: fathers in the families of the 1990s*. Children in Scotland. HMSO.

Carlson, B.E. (1982). Preschoolers' sex-role identity, father-role perception and paternal family participation. In Alduous, J. (ed.), *Two paychecks: life in dual earner families*. London: Sage Publications.

Catan, L. Dennison C. and Coleman, J., (1997). *Getting through: effective communication in the teenage years*. Trust for the Study of Adolescence and the BT Forum.

Central Statistical Office (1994). *Social focus on children*. HMSO.

Chase-Lansdale, P. L., Cherlin, A.J. and Kiernan, K.E. (1996). The long-term effects of parental divorce on the mental health of young adults: A developmental perspective. *Journal of Child Development*.

Cherlin, A.J., Furstenberg, F.F., Chase-Lansdale, P.L., Kiernan, K.E., Robins, P.K., Morrison, D.R. and Teieler, J.O. (1991). Longitudinal studies of effects of divorce on children in Great Britain and the United States. *Science*, 252.

Cherlin, A.J., Kiernan, K.E. and Chase-Lansdale, P.L. (1995). Parental divorce in childhood and demographic outcomes in young adulthood. *Demography*, 32, no. 3.

Child Poverty Action Group (1995a). *New figures show increase in child poverty*. Press release. 2 June.

Child Poverty Action Group (1995b). *Investing in a future for children*. London: Child Poverty Action Group.

Clarke, K., Glendinning, C. and Craig, G. (1996). *Small change*. Family and Parenthood series. London: Family Policy Studies Centre.

Clarke, L. (1996). Demographic change and the family situation of children. In Brannen, J. and O'Brien, M., *Children in families: research and policy*. Hove: Falmer Press.

Clarke, L. (1997). Unpublished analysis of 1991 National Child Development Study data.

Clarke, L. and Verropoulou, G. (1996). Unpublished results of modelling the risk of absent fathers. Social Statistics Research Unit. London: City University.

Clarke, L., Condy, A. and Downing, A. (1995). *Fathers: a socio-demographic profile*. Report to Department of Health. Family Policy Studies Centre Working Paper, 1997.

Clarke, L., Cooksey, E.C., Verropoulou, G. and Van Willigen, M. (1996a). *The experience of parenthood: fathers and mothers compared in Britain and the United States*. Paper presented to British Society for Population Studies Conference. University of St Andrew's.

Clarke, L., Joshi, H., Di Salvo, P. and Wright, J. (1997). *Stability and instability in children's family lives: longitudinal evidence from two British sources*. Centre for Population Studies Research. Paper 97-1. London School of Hygiene and Tropical Medicine.

Coleman, D. (1995). *Male fertility trends in industrial countries: theories in search of some evidence*. Paper presented to seminar on Fertility and the Male Life Cycle in the Era of Fertility Decline. Zacatecas, Mexico, 13-16 November 1995. Liège, Belgium: IUSSP.

Collier, R. (1995). *Masculinity, law and the family*. London: Routledge.

Collins, L. and Walton, P. (1995). Men behaving well. *Family Policy Studies Bulletin*. Family Policy Studies Centre. November.

Commission of the European Community (1991). The Eurobarometer: Lifestyles in the European Community. *Eurobarometer*, Issue 34, December.

Commission of the European Community (1993). The Europeans and the family. *Eurobarometer*, Issue 39, December.

Condy, A. and Roberts, C. (1994). FPSC 'Families and work' briefing. In Bayley, R., Condy, A. and Roberts, C. (eds.), *Policies for families: work, poverty and resources*. London: Family Policy Studies Centre.

Conference of European Ministers responsible for family affairs (1995). *The status and role of fathers: family policy aspects*. Secretariat memorandum, Council of Europe.

Cooksey, E.C. and Fondell, M.M. (1996). Spending time with his kids: Effects of family structure on fathers' and children's lives. *Journal of Marriage and the Family*. no. 58.

Cooper, C. and Lewis, S. (1995). *Beyond family friendly organisations*. The seven million project. Working paper 2. DEMOS.

Craig, G., Glendinning, C. and Clarke, K. (1996). Policy on the hoof: The British Child Support Act in practice. In May, M., Brunsdon, E. and Craig, G. (eds.), *Social Policy Review 8*. Social Policy Association.

Cretney, S. and Mason, J. (1990). *Principles of family law*. London: Sweet and Maxwell.

Daniels, L. (1995). Parents at work. In Bayley, R., Condy, A. and Roberts, C. (eds.), *Policies for families: work, poverty and resources*, Proceedings of seminars held in 1994. London: Family Policy Studies Centre.

Davies, R., Elias, P. and Penn, R. (1992). The relationship between a husband's employment and his wife's participation in the labour force. *Oxford Bulletin of Economics and Statistics*.

Dearden, K., Hale, C. and Blankson, M. (1994). Family structure, function and the early transition to fatherhood in Great Britain: Identifying antecedents using longitudinal data. *Journal of Marriage and the Family*, 56.

Dench, G. (1994). *The frog and the prince and the problem of men*. Neanderthal Books.

Dench, G. (1996a). Exploring variations in men's family roles. *Findings*, Social Policy Research 99. York: Joseph Rowntree Foundation.

Dench, G. (1996b). *The place of men in changing family values*. London: Institute of Community Studies.

Dennis, N. (1993). *Rising crime and the dismembered family*. London: Institute of Economic Affairs.

Dennis, N. and Erdos, G. (1992). *Families without fatherhood*. London: Institute of Economic Affairs.

Department for Education and Employment (1997). *Labour Market Trends*, March.

Department of Social Security (1995a). *Social security statistics 1995*. HMSO.

Department of Social Security (1995b). *Households below average income: a statistical analysis 1979 to 1991/92*. HMSO.

Department of Social Security (1995c). Households below average income statistics published. Press release. 14 July.

Department of Social Security (1995d). *Tax benefit model tables: April 1995*. Analytical Services Division. HMSO.

Department of Social Security (1996). *Child Support Agency: quarterly summary of statistics. May 1996*. Analytical Services Division, Government Statistical Service.

Department of Social Security (1997). *Child Support Agency: quarterly summary of statistics. November 1996*. Analytical Services Division, Government Statistical Service.

Department of Trade and Industry (1996). Consultation document, *Annex C. EC Working Time Directive – compliance cost assessment*. DTI

Dewar, J. and Parker, S. (1992). *Law and the family*. London: Butterworths.

Dex, S. and Taylor, M. (1994). Household employment in 1991. *Employment Gazette*. October.

Dex, S., Taylor, M. and Clark, A. (1995). *Household labour supply: report on the employment of household members in wave 1 of the British Household Panel Study*. ED Research Brief. Employment Department.

Di Salvo, P., Clarke, L. and Joshi, H. (1996). *Longitudinal perspectives on family change: mothers, fathers and children*. Paper submitted for publication.

Dickens, R., Fry, V. and Pashardes, P. (1995). *The cost of children and the welfare state*. Findings, Social Policy Research 89. York: Joseph Rowntree Foundation.

van Dongen, M.C.P. (1995). Men's aspirations concerning child care: The extent to which they are realised. In van Dongen, M.C.P., Frinking, G.A.B. and Jacobs, M.J.G. (eds.), *Changing fatherhood: an interdisciplinary perspective*. Amsterdam: Thesis Publisher.

Douglas, G. and Lowe, N. (1993). Becoming a parent in English law. In Eekelaar, J. and Sarcevic, P. (eds.), *Modern Society*. Lancaster: Kluwer Academic Publishers.

Eekelaar, J. and Maclean, M. (eds.) (1994). *A reader on family law*. Oxford University Press.

Elias, P. and Gregory, M. (1994). *The changing structure of occupations and earnings in Great Britain, 1975-1990: an analysis based on the New Earnings Survey Panel Dataset*. Research Series No. 27. Employment Department.

Elliott, B.J. and Richards, M.P.M. (1991). Children and divorce: Educational performance and behaviour before and after parental separation. *International Journal of Law and the Family*.

Employment Committee (1995a). *Mothers in employment. Vol. 1: report and proceedings of the Committee*. First report. Session 1994-95, HC 227-1. HMSO.

Employment Committee (1995b). *Mothers in employment: government reply to the first report of the Committee in session 1994-95*. Second special report, HC 457. HMSO.

Employment Gazette (1995).

European Commission (1996). *The organisation of working time*. Information Sheet IS/S/1.96.

European Commission Network on Childcare (1996). *A review of services for young children in the European Union 1990-1995*. European Commission Directorate General V (Employment, Industrial Relations and Social Affairs). Equal Opportunities Unit.

Eurostat (1996). *Labour Force Survey results 1995*. Office for Official Publications of the European Community.

Exploring Parenthood (1995). Developing work and family services in the workplace. *Findings*, Social Policy Research 69. York: Joseph Rowntree Foundation.

Family Policy Studies Centre (1994) *Families and the law*. Family Report 1. London.

Farrington, D. (1994). The influence of the family on delinquent development. In Henricson, C. (ed.), *Crime and the family*. Conference report. Proceedings of an international conference held in London. February. London: Family Policy Studies Centre

Farrington, D. (1996). *Understanding and preventing youth crime*. York: York Publishing Services Ltd.

Fathers in families of tomorrow (1993). Danish Ministry of Social Affairs and European Commission.

Ferri, E. (1993). *Life at 33: The fifth follow-up of the National Child Development Study*. London: National Children's Bureau and City University.

Ferri, E. (1994). *Parenthood at 33: Early findings from the fifth sweep of the National Child Development Study.* Unpublished paper.

Ferri, E. and Smith, K. (1996). *Parenting in the 1990s.* Family and Parenthood series. London: Family Policy Studies Centre.

Financial Times (1995). Parental leave plan for EU social chapter.

Gershuny, J. (1995a). Relationships between women's employment and other activities. In Bayley, R., Condy, A. and Roberts, C. (eds.), *Policies for families: work, poverty and resources.* London: Family Policy Studies Centre.

Gershuny, J. (1995b). Time Keynsianism. In The time squeeze. *Demos Quarterly.*

Gershuny, J. (1996). Unpublished data. ESRC Research Centre on Micro-Social Change. University of Essex.

Gershuny, J. and Robinson, J.P. (1988). Historical changes in the household division of labour. *Demography*, 25/4, November.

Ghate, D. and Daniels, A. *Talking about my generation. A survey of 8-15 year olds growing up in the 1990s.* London: NSPCC.

Goodman, A. and Webb, S. (1994). *For richer, for poorer: The changing distribution of income in the United Kingdom, 1961-91.* London: Institute for Fiscal Studies.

Gregg, P. (1995). More work in fewer households. In Bayley, J., Condy, A. and Roberts, C. (eds.), *Policies for families: work, poverty and resources.* Proceedings of seminars held in 1994. London: Family Policy Studies Centre.

Gregg, P. and Wadsworth, J. (1996). *Mind the gap, please? The changing nature of entry jobs in Britain.* Centre for Economic Performance. Discussion Paper no. 303. London School of Economics.

Guardian (1994). Tory MPs risk row over paternity leave. 27 September.

Halsey, A.H. (1992). In Dennis, N. and Erdos, G., *Families without fatherhood.* London: Institute of Economic Affairs.

Harkness, S. (1996). Unpublished data on shares of family income by family type. Suntory-Toyota International Centre for Economics and Related Disciplines. London School of Economics.

Harkness, S., Machin, S. and Waldfogel, J. (1995). *Evaluating the pin money hypothesis: the relationship between women's labour market activity, family income and poverty in Britain.* Welfare State Programme. Discussion paper 108. Suntory-Toyota International Centre for Economics and Related Disciplines. London School of Economics.

Harrop, A. and Moss, P. (1994). Working parents: Trends in the 1980s. *Employment Gazette*, October.

Haskey, J. (1990). Children in families broken by divorce. *Population Trends.* no. 61. HMSO.

Haskey, J. (1993). Lone parents and married parents with dependent children in Great Britain. *Population Trends.* no. 72. HMSO.

Haskey, J. (1994). Estimated numbers of one-parent families and their prevalence in Great Britain in 1991. *Population trends.* no. 78. HMSO.

Hawkins, A.J. and Eggebeen, D.J. (1991). Are fathers fungible? Patterns of co-resident adult men in maritally disrupted families and young children's well-being. *Journal of Marriage and the Family*, 53, 958-72.

Henwood, M., Rimmer, L. and Wicks, M. (1987, reprinted 1992). *Inside the family: changing roles of men and women.* London: Family Policy Studies Centre.

Hershman, D. (1993). Parental Responsibility Orders and contact applications by unmarried fathers. *Family Law*, February. Jordan Publishing.

Hewitt, P. (1993). *About time: the revolution in work and family life*. London: Institute of Public Policy Research.

Hills, J. (1995). *Income and Wealth. vol. 2*. York: Joseph Rowntree Foundation.

Hipgrave, T. (1982). Lone fatherhood: a problematic status. In McKee, L. and O'Brien, M. (eds.), *The father figure*. London: Tavistock Publications.

Hochschild, A.R. (1995). Understanding the future of fatherhood. The 'daddy hierarchy' and beyond. In van Dongen, M.C.P. *et al.* (eds.), *Changing fatherhood: An interdisciplinary perspective*. Amsterdam: Thesis Publisher.

Hogg, L. and Harker, L. (1992). *The family friendly employer: Examples from Europe*, Daycare Trust in association with Families and Work Institute, New York.

Holtermann, S. (1995). *All our futures: The impact of public expenditure and fiscal policies on Britain's children and young people*. London: Barnardos.

Holtermann, S. and Clarke, K. (1992). *Parents, employment rights and childcare*. Manchester: Equal Opportunities Commission.

Industrial Relations Services (1994). *Paternity Leave*, Equal Opportunities Review, No. 55, May/June, London: Industrial Relations Services.

Jackson, S. (1987). Great Britain. In Lamb, M.E., *The father's role in cross-cultural perspectives*. John Wiley and Sons Inc.

Joseph Rowntree Foundation findings (1994). Women's pay and family income equality. Social Policy Research 60.

Joseph Rowntree Foundation (1995). *Inquiry into income and wealth. vol. 1*. York: Joseph Rowntree Foundation.

Joshi, H. (1996). *The opportunity costs of childbearing: More than mothers' business*. Lecture to British Society for Population Studies. St Andrews.

Joshi, H., Dale, A., Ward, C. and Davies, H. (1995). *Dependence and independence in the finances of women aged 33*. Family and Parenthood series. London: Family Policy Studies Centre.

Journal of Family Issues (1994). Fatherhood: Results from national surveys. 15:1.

Junger-Tas, J. (1994). The changing family and its relationship with delinquent behaviour. In Henricson, C. (ed.), *Crime and the family*. Conference report. Proceedings of international conference, London. London: Family Policy Studies Centre.

Kiernan, K.E. (1992a). Men and women at work and at home. In Jowell, R. *et al.* (eds.), *British social attitudes: The 9th report*. Social and Community Planning Research. Aldershot: Dartmouth.

Kiernan, K.E. (1992b). The impact of family disruption in childhood on transitions made in young adult life. *Population Studies*, 46, 213-34.

Kiernan, K.E. (1995a). *Transitions to parenthood: Young mothers, young fathers: associated factors and later life experiences*. Welfare State Programme Paper no. 113. Suntory-Toyota International Centre for Economics and Related Disciplines. London School of Economics.

Kiernan, K.E. (1995b). Social backgrounds and post-birth experiences of young parents. *Findings*, Social Policy Research 80. Joseph Rowntree Foundation.

Kraemer, S. (1988). Fathers. Tavistock Clinic public lecture. Tavistock Clinic paper no. 93.

Kraemer, S. (1993). Fathers' roles: Research findings and policy implications. Tavistock Clinic public lecture. Tavistock Clinic paper no. 142.

Kraemer, S. (1995a). What are fathers for? In Burck, C. and Speed, B., *Gender, power and relationships*. London: Routledge.

Kraemer, S. (1995b). *Parenting yesterday, today and tomorrow*. Families and Parenting Conference. London: Family Policy Studies Centre.

Kraemer, S. (1995c). A man's place? In Clulow, C. (ed.), *Women, men and marriage: Talks from the Tavistock Marital Studies Institute*. London: Sheldon Press.

Kraemer, S. (1995d). *Active fathering for the future*. The seven million project. Working paper 7. DEMOS.

Lamb, M.E. (1981). *The role of fathers in child development*. John Wiley and Sons Inc, 2nd edition.

Lamb, M.E. (1995). Paternal influences on child development. In van Dongen, M.C.P., Frinking, G.A.B. and Jacobs, M.J.G. (1995). *Changing fatherhood: An interdisciplinary perspective*. Amsterdam: Thesis Publisher.

Lamb, M.E. (1996). *What are fathers for?* Presentation at Men and Their Children conference. Institute for Public Policy Research.

Law Commission (1982). *Illegitimacy*. Law Commission no. 118.

Law Commission (1986). *Illegitimacy Second Report*, Law Commission no. 157.

Lewis, C. (1982). The observation of father-infant relationships: An 'attachment' to outmoded concepts. In McKee, L. and O'Brien, M., *The father figure*. London: Tavistock Publications.

Lewis, C. (1986). *Becoming a father*. Buckingham: Open University Press.

Lewis, C. (1993). Mothers' and fathers' roles: Similar or different? In *Fathers in families of tomorrow*. Danish Ministry of Social Affairs and European Commission.

Lewis, C. (1995a). A comment on van Dongen, M.C.P., Men's aspirations concerning child care: The extent to which they are realised. In van Dongen, M.C.P. *et al.* (eds.), *Changing fatherhood: An interdisciplinary perspective*. Amsterdam: Thesis Publisher.

Lewis, C. (1995b). In conclusion: What opportunities are open to fathers? In Moss, P. (ed.), *Father figures: Fathers in the families of the 1990s*. Children in Scotland. HMSO.

Lewis, C. (1996). Fathers and preschoolers. In Lamb, M.E. (ed.), *The role of the father in child development*. John Wiley and Sons Inc.

Lewis, C. and O'Brien, M. (1987). *Reassessing fatherhood: New observations on fathers and the modern family*. London: Sage Publications.

Lloyd, T. (1995). Fathers in the media: An analysis of newspaper coverage of fathers. In Moss, P. (ed.), *Father figures: Fathers in the families of the 1990s*, Children in Scotland. HMSO.

Lord Chancellor's Department (1995). *Judicial Statistics 1994*. HMSO.

Lummis, T. (1982). The historical dimension of fatherhood: A case study 1890-1914. In McKee, L. and O'Brien, M., *The father figure*. London: Tavistock Publications.

Machin, S. and Waldfogel, J. (1994). The decline of the male breadwinner. *Changing shares of husbands' and wives' earnings in family income*. Welfare State Programme, WSP/103. STICERD. London School of Economics.

Maclean, M. (1996). *Financial obligations of parenthood: Rules and choices*. Centre for Socio-Legal Studies, Oxford. Paper presented at Sociological Studies Association. March.

McAllister, F. (1995). *Marital breakdown and the health of the nation*. London: One plus One.

McKee, L. and O'Brien, M. (eds.) (1982). *The father figure*. London: Tavistock Publications.

McRae, S. and Daniel, W.W. (1991). *Maternity rights: The experience of women and employers*. First findings. Policy Studies Institute.

McRae, S. (1993). *Cohabiting mothers: Changing mothers and motherhood*. London: Policy Studies Institute.

Marsh, A., Ford, R. and Finlayson, L. (1997). *Lone parents, work and benefits*. Department of Social Security. Research Report No. 61. The Stationery Office.

Martin, J. and Roberts, C. (1984). *Women and employment: A lifetime perspective*. HMSO.

Meltzer, H. (1994). *Day care services for children: A survey carried out on behalf of the Department of Health in 1990*. Office of Population Censuses and Surveys. HMSO.

Millar, J. and Glendinning, C. (1987). Invisible women, invisible poverty. In Glendinning, C. and Millar, J., *Women and Poverty in Britain*. Wheatsheaf.

Morgan, P. (1995). *Farewell to the family? Public policy and family breakdown in Britain and the USA*. Institute for Economic Affairs.

Morrison, D.R. and Cherlin, A.J. (1995). The divorce process and young children's well-being: A prospective analysis. *Journal of Marriage and the Family*, 57, 800-812.

Moss, P. (1994). Taking the gender out of leave. *Family Policy Bulletin*, December.

Moss, P. (ed.) (1995). *Father figures: Fathers in the families of the 1990s*. Children in Scotland. HMSO.

Moss, P. (1996). *Men and their children: An EU perspective*. Institute for Public Policy Research Conference.

Mott, F.L. (1994). Sons, daughters and fathers' absence: Differentials in father-leaving probabilities and in home environments. *Journal of Family Issues* 'Fatherhood: results from national surveys', 15:1.

Mulgan, G. and Wilkinson, H. (1995). Well-being and time. *Demos Quarterly*, 'The time squeeze', Issue 5.

National Opinion Poll (1995). *Sixty minute father*. Market research report.

New Ways to Work (1995). *Balanced lives: changing work patterns for men*. London.

Newson, J. and Newson, E. (1963). *Infant care in an urban community*. London: George Allen and Unwin Ltd.

Ní Bhrolcháin, M., Chappell, R. and Diamond, I. (1994). *Educational and socio-demographic outcomes among the children of disrupted and intact marriages*. Department of Social Statistics, University of Southampton.

O'Brien, M. (1982). The working father. In Beaile, N. and McGuire, J. (eds.), *Fathers: Psychological perspective*. Junction Books.

O'Brien, M. (1995). Fatherhood and family policies in Europe. In Hantrais, L. and Letablier, M.-T. (eds.), *The family in social policy and family policy. Cross-national research papers*. ESRC and CNAF.

O'Brien, M. and Jones, D. (1995). Young people's attitudes to fatherhood. In Moss, P. (ed.), *Father figures: Fathers in the families of the 1990s*. Children in Scotland. HMSO.

O'Brien, M. and Jones, D. (1996). The absence and presence of fathers: Accounts from children's diaries. In Bjornberg, U. and Kollind, A.-K. (eds.), *Men's family relations*. Gothenburg: University of Göteborg Publications.

OECD (1992). *Unemployment compensation schemes in OECD countries*. Employment Outlook. OECD.

Office of Population Censuses and Surveys (1995a). *Birth statistics 1993*. Series FM1. HMSO.

Office of Population Censuses and Surveys (1995b). *General Household Survey 1993*. HMSO.

Office of Population Censuses and Surveys (1995c). *Marriage and Divorce Statistics 1993*. Series FM2. HMSO.

Office of Population Censuses and Surveys (1996). *Living in Britain: Results from the 1994 General Household Survey*. HMSO.

Office of Population Censuses and Surveys (1997). *Living in Britain: Results from the 1995 General Household Survey*. HMSO.

Orbach, S. (1994). Is dad a boy's best friend? *Guardian Weekend*, June.

Pappenheim, K. (1997). 'The family' budget leaves one in five children worse off. *Family Policy Bulletin*. London: Family Policy Studies Centre.

Parker, H. (1995). *Taxes, benefits and family life: The seven deadly traps*. Research monograph 50. Institute of Economic Affairs.

Parmenter, J. (1993). *Looking after baby: Yesterday, today … tomorrow: Trends in infant care practice. Bristol 1951-1991*. Redcliffe Press.

Pleck, J.H. (1986). Employment and fatherhood: issues and innovative policies. In Lamb, M.E. (ed.), *The fathers' role: Applied perspectives*. John Wiley and Sons Inc.

Priest, J. (1995). The putative father under Rules of Court. *Family Law*, February. Jordan Publishing.

Rendall, M. R., Clarke, L., Peters, E.P., Ranjit, N. and Verropoulou, G. (1996). *Retrospective and panel underreporting of male fertility in the United States and Britain*. Paper presented at Essex Centre for Microsocial Change. Working paper available from Rendall at Cornell University, Ithaca, New York.

Richards, M. (1982). How should we approach the study of fathers? In McKee, L. and O'Brien, M. (1982), *The father figure*. London: Tavistock Publications.

Ringen, S. and Halpin, B. (1995). *The standard of living of children*. Department of Applied Social Studies and Social Research, University of Oxford.

Roberts, C.M. (1996). Private communication with senior member of Conservative government, November 1996.

Ruhm, C. and Teague, J. (1995). *Parental leave policies in Europe and North America*. Working paper 5065. US National Bureau of Economic Research.

Russell, G. (1983). *The changing role of fathers*. Queensland: Open University Press.

Sainsbury 's. The family is fine, but under pressure. *The Magazine*, May 1994.

Samuels, A. (1996) quoted in David Cohen, It's a guy thing. *Guardian Weekend*, 4 May.

Sarre, S. (1996). *A place for fathers: Fathers and social policy in the post-War period*. Welfare State Programme, WSP/125. Suntory-Toyota International Centre for Economics and Related Disciplines. London School of Economics.

Saunders, G. and Smailes, D. (1996). *Tolley's Income Tax 1996-97*. London: Tolley Publishing Co. Ltd.

Scott, J. (1990). Women and the family. In Jowell, R., Witherspoon, S. and Brook, L. (eds.), *British social attitudes: The 7th report*. Social and Community Planning Research. London: Duckworth.

Scott, J., Braun, M. and Alwin, D. (1993). The family way. In Jowell, R., Brook, L. and Dowds, L. (eds.), *International Social Attitudes: The 10th BSA report*. Social and Community Planning Research. London: Duckworth.

Seltzer, J.A. (1995). Relationships between fathers and children who live apart. *Journal of Marriage and the Family*, 52, 79-101.

Sianne, G. and Wilkinson, H. (1995). Are the old gender battles being replaced by a new partnership? *Guardian*.

Simpson, B. (1994). Access and child contact centres in England and Wales: An ethnographic perspective. *Children and Society*, 8, no.1.

Simpson, B., McCarthy, P. and Walker, J. (1995). *Being there: Fathers after divorce*. Relate Centre for Family Studies, University of Newcastle-upon-Tyne.

Smith, H.L. and Morgan, S.P. (1994). Children's closeness to father as reported by mothers, sons and daughters, *Journal of Family Issues*. 'Fatherhood: results from national surveys', 15:1.

Social Security Committee (1995a). *Low income statistics: Low income families 1989-1992*. First report. House of Commons, 254. HMSO.

Social Security Committee (1995b). *Review of expenditure on social security*. Third report, 132. HMSO.

Social Trends 1995 (1995). Office of Population Censuses and Surveys. HMSO.

Social Trends 1996 (1996) Office of Population Censuses and Surveys. HMSO.

Speak, S. (1996) 'What about Dads?' Presentation at Trust for the Study of Adolescence conference, *Understanding teenage parents: what current research has to say*.

Speed, M. and Kent, N. (1996) *Child Support Agency National Client Satisfaction Survey 1995*. Child Support Agency. HMSO.

Starrels, M.E. (1994). Gender differences in parent-child relations, *Journal of Family Issues*.

Sweeting, H. and West, P. (1996). *The relationship between family life and young people's lifestyles*. Findings, Social Policy Research 95. York: Joseph Rowntree Foundation.

Thomson, K. (1995). Working mothers: Choice or circumstance?' In Jowell, R., Curtice, J., Park, A., Brook, L. and Ahrendt, D., *British Social Attitudes: The 12th Report*. Social and Community Planning Research. Aldershot: Dartmouth.

Trades Union Congress (1996a). *Underworked and underpaid: A report on young people's labour market experiences*. Economic and Social Affairs Department. Trades Union Congress.

Trades Union Congress (1996b). *Parental leave: A TUC guide to the European Parental Leave Agreement*. Equal Rights Department, Trades Union Congress.

Tyrell, B. (1995). Time in our lives: Facts and analysis on the 90s. *Demos Quarterly*, 'The time squeeze', Issue 5.

United Nations (1994). *Reinventing fatherhood*. Occasional Paper series no. 14. International Year of the Family 1994. United Nations.

Utting, D. (1995). *Family and parenthood: supporting families, preventing breakdown*. York: Joseph Rowntree Foundation.

Utting, D., Bright, J. and Henricson, C. (1993). *Crime and the Family: Improving child-rearing and preventing delinquency*. Occasional Paper 16. London: Family Policy Studies Centre.

Wasik, M. and Taylor, R. (1993). *Blackstone's guide to the Criminal Justice Act 1991*. Blackstone's.

Watson, G. (1992). Hours of work in Great Britain and Europe. *Employment Gazette*. Employment Department.

Watson, G. (1994). The flexible workforce and patterns of working hours in the UK. *Employment Gazette*. Employment Department.

Webb, S. (1994). Hearing 3: Families, poverty and resources. In *All-Party Parliamentary Group on Parenting and International Year of the Family UK. Parliamentary Hearing* (1994). All-Party Parliamentary Group on Parenting and International Year of the Family UK.

Wheelock, J. (1990). *Husbands at home: The domestic economy in a post-industrial society*. London: Routledge.

Wilkinson, H. and Briscoe, I. (1996). *Parental leave: The price of family values*. Project report. Demos.

Wilkinson, H. and Mulgan, G. (1995). *Freedom's children: Work, relationships and politics for 18-34 year olds in Britain today*. Demos.

Witherspoon, S. (1985). Sex roles and gender issues. In Jowell, R. and Witherspoon, S. (eds.), *British social attitudes: The 1985 report*. Social and Community Planning Research. Aldershot: Gower.

Witherspoon, S. (1988). Interim report: A woman's work. In Jowell, R. *et al.* (eds.), *British social attitudes: The 5th report*. Social and Community Planning Research. Aldershot: Gower.

Young, M. and Halsey, A.H. (1995). *Family and community socialism*. London: Institute for Public Policy Research.